796.52
L892 g

4/06

W9-BGU-568

GUIDE TO
CLIMBING

0 11557 00152 5

GUIDE TO
CLIMBING

Tony Lourens

STACKPOLE
BOOKS

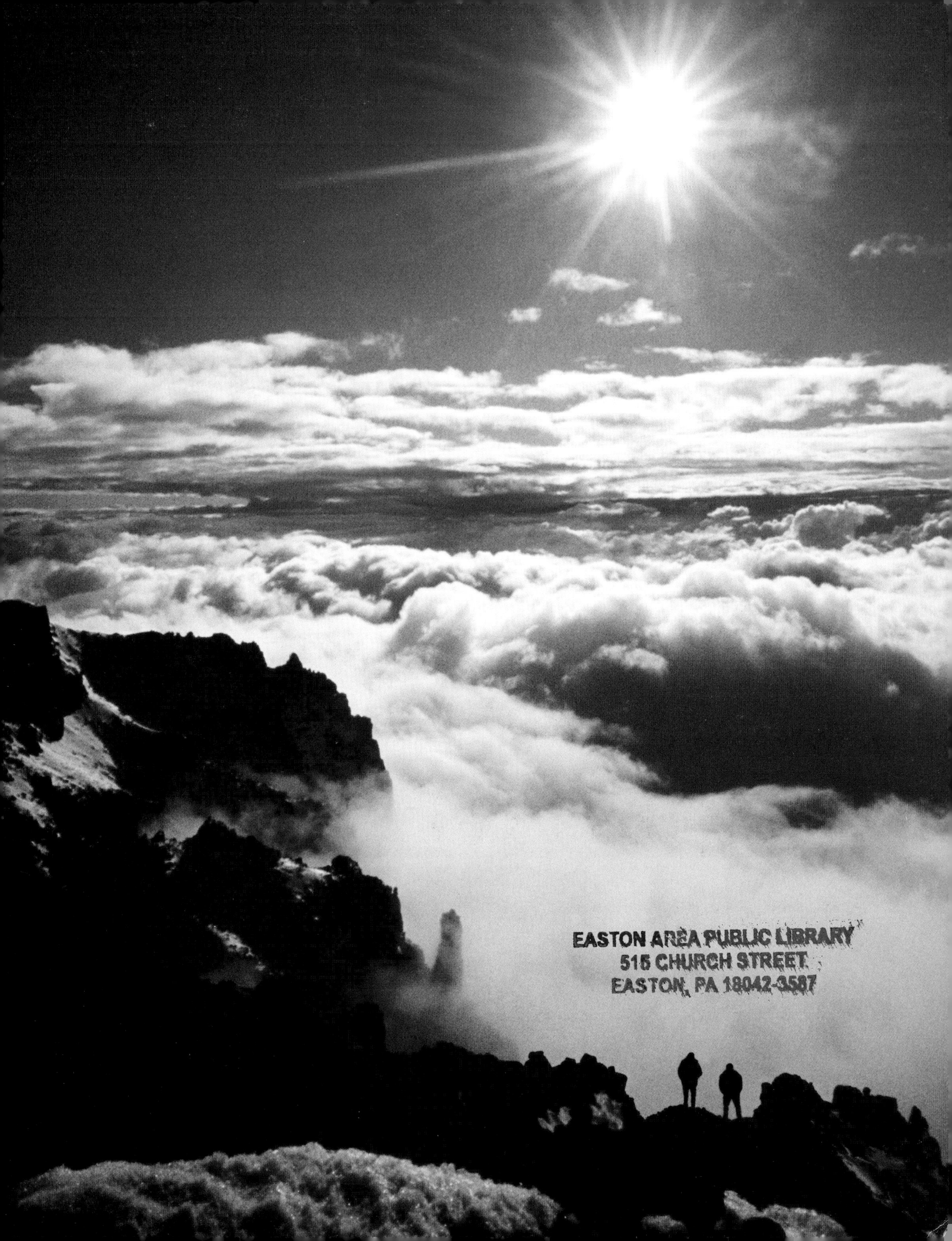

First published in 2005 by
New Holland (Publishers) Ltd
London • Cape Town • Sydney • Auckland

Printed in Malaysia

10 9 8 7 6 5 4 3 2 1

First edition

Library of Congress Cataloging-in-Publication Data
on file with the Library of Congress
ISBN 0-8117-0152-2
ISBN 978-0-8117-0152-5

No book is a substitute for experience itself. It is recommended that this book be used in conjunction with
learning from an experienced climber.
The author and publishers have made every effort to ensure that the information contained in this book
was correct at the time of going to press. They accept no responsibility for any loss, injury or inconvenience
sustained by any person using this book or the advice given within it.

Opposite: *High on the limestone walls of a typically exposed route in an setting that is unmistakably Thailand.*

Previous page: *Above the clouds on Mount Kilimanjaro.*

Title page: *Jumaring on the Central Tower of the Torres del Paine in Patagonia.*

CONTENTS

Introduction

Rock types and terrain

Equipment and gear

Essential skills and techniques

Ropework and belay

Traditional (trad) and wall climbing

Sport climbing

Bouldering and solo climbing

Indoor climbing and competitions

Mixed alpine and Himalayan climbing

Ice and waterfalls

Preparation and training

Emergency procedures

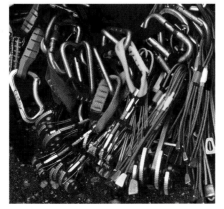

INTRODUCTION

Climbing is a form of escapism that takes you to the most beautiful parts of the world. While you are climbing your concentration is absolute; no other thoughts have a hope of breaking through that barrier. It is also about having fun in a healthy environment. There are no rules or regulations and the only competition is the rock. Ability is neither here nor there, because one can climb at any level and still have a thoroughly good time. In its simplest form, climbing involves scrambling over boulders or up easy rock steps. On the other side of the scale it is a precise and carefully calculated game that demands tiptop physical strength and fitness, precise technique and, above all, a positive mental approach. It is not just about climbing from point A to point B. It is a vertical chess game that can pose many questions and bring many surprises.

The allure of climbing

Climbing is about one person's ability pitted against a problem posed by a section of rock (or mountain). If you fail to solve the riddle the first time (as is often the case), then you have to analyze your attempt and perhaps change your strategy.

What a feeling it is to move fluently and smoothly over rock, to feel your fingers slot neatly into a crack, or to pull down on positive holds up steep rock, solving sequences as you progress. It is like choreographed ballet on a vertical plane. But it doesn't end there. Sitting around a fire at your campsite that night, the moon reflecting a gentle light across the lake and illuminating the rock walls of the valley, your muscles tired and your tendons aching, all you want to talk about is the climbing of the day. That particular series of moves that you eventually pieced together, or the route that you want to try tomorrow or future climbing trips with people who have the same passion and emotions as you. This is what makes people give up everything to follow a life of climbing; to hit the road and take tomorrow as it comes; climbing as a way of life.

Above: Ian Howell prepares the evening brew at 2600m (8,500 feet) altitude, just below Monte Perdido in the Spanish Pyrenées.

'Many a time I have sat on the summit after a difficult climb, ravenous, my nerves worn out, my strength exhausted, but blissfully happy. It is that feeling which drives us climbers ever and again up into the high mountain tracts, remote from all life; which impels us to undertake the most fearful exertions, which drives us far beyond the narrow confines of the world.'

Nanga Parbat Pilgrimage
by Hermann Bühl

Left: A 19th century photograph from WE Davidson's Album of Alpine Guides and Mountaineers, showing a party of six climbing a slab.

History

It is generally accepted that alpinism originated with the ascent of Mont Blanc in 1786 by Michel Gabriel Paccard and Jacques Balmat. The sport grew, culminating nearly 150 years later with Himalayan exploration in the form of very large expeditions using siege tactics to conquer the world's highest peaks, all of which fell in the space of 14 years between 1950 and 1964.

Alpine climbing advanced slowly at first, then more rapidly as better equipment was developed and more progressive techniques were used. It was really in the early to mid 20th century when most of the more important ascents took place in the Alps. Climbers like Emilio Comici, Ricardo Cassin and later Walter Bonatti were at the forefront of the action and made first ascents of routes like the North Face of the Cima Grande, Walker Spur, South West Pillar of the Petit Dru and many others. These routes were regarded as the most difficult in world mountaineering at the time and are still considered as serious undertakings for experienced climbers.

If alpine climbing started so far back, rock climbing in its pure form has a much shorter history. Some say it started with the ascent of the Eastern Terrace of Clogwynn D'ur Arddu, Snowdon, in Wales by two botanists, Reverends W Bingley and P Williams. Others say that true rock climbing began with the ascent of a Lakeland pinnacle called Pillar about 1826. Many still pinpoint the birth of true rock climbing to the ascent of another Lakeland pinnacle called Napes Needle in 1886. But a year earlier, at the tip of the African continent, Gustav Nefdt climbed the formidable western tower of Towerkop above the town of Ladismith in South Africa. This was a remarkable feat that was rated as the hardest climb of the time and 64 years passed before it saw a second ascent. As with alpinism, pure rock climbing evolved quickly through the 20th century. Yosemite Valley in California, USA, became one of the most important areas in the world for hard climbing. Many of the big and seemingly impenetrable walls of the valley began to fall to repeated attempts by a number of climbers who made the valley their home. Climbers like John Salathé, Warren Harding, Royal Robbins, Tom Frost and later Jim Bridwell pioneered some of the most important and advanced rock climbs in the world. Some climbers even forged their own rudimentary equipment to deal specifically with the crack systems that were so unique to Yosemite. The valley played an important role in the 1960s and 70s, and is still considered by many to be the world's top traditional (trad) climbing area, hosting an enormous amount of big wall routes in an impressive setting.

Above left: *Pitch 14 of Zodiac on the 450m (1500ft) route on El Capitan, Yosemite. The valley features largely in the history of climbing.*

Above right: *Notes from the Underground is one of the many 'trad' routes in the Yosemite Valley. El Capitan is in the background.*

Modern practices

Climbing has come a long way from the days when the given wisdom was that 'the leader never falls'. Modern ropes and equipment have made it possible to push the limits far beyond what was thought possible a mere 30 or 40 years ago.

Besides body harnesses and sticky rubber soles, one of the most important breakthroughs was the advent of the camming device in 1978. Invented by Ray Jardine, they caused grades to soar, and many crack lines previously considered 'unprotectable' (lack of protection for the climber) could be climbed in relative safety.

Some climbers are never satisfied with existing routes; there is the urge to pioneer new lines, create harder routes, free old aid (artificially climbed) climbs and climb higher and more remote walls. Equipment manufacturers realize this, so are continually designing and inventing gear to make it possible to push ever deeper into the realm of the 'impossible'.

Another piece of hardware that allowed climbers to ascend blank faces, was the bolt. First used to provide protection on sections between crack systems, bolts were used increasingly to allow largely unprotected faces to be climbed.

This practice evolved fairly quickly into what is now known as sport climbing. The French were really the main developers of sport climbing in the earlier years. They

put up thousands of routes using previously unaccepted styles, like pre-inspection of the routes and bolting of routes on abseil (rappel). Purists felt this was unethical, but the practice spread quickly and by now climbers from all climbing nations will have clipped some bolts.

Above: A climber is shown attempting a steep and technically demanding sport route. This form of climbing has pre-placed, fixed protection points at regular intervals up the rock face. The climber attaches quickdraws to these and the rope is threaded through them. In this way any fall is arrested by the last bolt that was 'clipped.'

Above: Mallory and Irvine leaving Camp 4, on their 1924 Everest Expedition (photographed by Noel Odell). Mallory, who coined the phrase 'Because it's there' in response to the question why they wanted to climb Mt Everest, is on the left.

Left Climbers scale the slopes of a Himalayan peak without the use of supplemental oxygen, but with modern clothing, sleeping bags and tents made of hi tech fabrics.

Today more people are actively involved in sport climbing than any other discipline of mountaineering, purely because it is safer than other forms of climbing, demands less time and it's a great deal of fun. It also allows for much harder grades to be climbed, since it obviates concerns about placing protection.

Besides technical hardware, advances in synthetic fabric manufacture have also made a difference. Today's top climbers may well shun the use of supplemental oxygen as an artificial aid that gives an unfair advantage when climbing 8000m (26,000ft) peaks. However, their superbly designed and very warm clothing, sleeping bags and tents made of hi tech fabrics make an enormous difference in keeping warm, which is important in warding off frostbite and altitude sickness. Climbing high without supplemental oxygen is a different story if you only have a pile of sheep skins for protection.

Types of climbing

Climbing encompasses many different sports undertaken in the mountains. Very few climbers partake in the full range of activities that constitute climbing. What follows is a closer look at the different disciplines.

ALPINE

The term alpine stems from the mountain range that runs through central Europe – the Alps, where curious and adventurous natives of the surrounding countryside first ventured onto the slopes of these snowy giants and later started conquering the higher peaks. Climbing most routes in the Alps generally involves climbing on rock, snow and sometimes ice (known as mixed ground); in remote areas with long and complex descents; contending with objective dangers like crevasses, avalanche risks and cold temperatures; and keeping a close watch on the weather. Over the years, the term alpine has become accepted worldwide to describe climbing that involves all, or some of these attributes and the style it requires.

Himalayan peaks are also climbed alpine-style these days – when the route is ascended in one push by a party of climbers carrying everything they need, as opposed to the siege tactics of old.

HIMALAYAN

The Himalayan mountain range is a colossal collection of peaks, passes and glaciers that form a barrier across the Asian continent between India and Central Asia, Tibet and China. It extends over 2000km (1250 miles), with peaks of between 7000m (23,000ft) and 8800m (29,000ft) in height. The world's 14 highest peaks are all situated in the Greater Himalayan Range, including the world's highest point, Mt Everest, at 8848m (29,030ft).

When Westerners first started climbing in the Himalayas, they soon realized that the extremely high altitudes required a new style of climbing. So they developed siege tactics. With the help of local porters to carry tons of equipment and supplies, they could establish camps higher and higher up the mountain; retreating to base camp to recover and then reascending to stocked camps, pushing ever higher until it was possible to go for the summit in a final push.

Apart from the siege tactics, the actual nature of the climbing is similar to alpine climbing, but on a much grander scale – with more serious objective dangers and at a substantially higher altitude.

Above: *Alpinists in the French Alps, on the Mont Blanc Massif, pause at La Junction, the confluence of the Géant Glacier with the Mer du Glace. The 4013m (13,000ft) Dent du Géant rises at centre with the Géant Icefall on the right.*

ROCK CLIMBING

Rock climbing covers a wide variety of styles and techniques. The different disciplines are traditional (trad)-, sport-, free-, aid-, solo- and big wall climbing.

Traditional (trad) climbing. A route (single or multipitch) is climbed from the ground up. Traditional equipment is placed in cracks, cavities and pockets. Rope is threaded through these to protect the climber in the event of a fall. The gear is placed by the leader as each section of rock is climbed. Such a section is commonly known as a pitch, which is usually between 20m (66ft) and 60m (200ft) in length. When the leader reaches a suitable stance (*see glossary*) for an anchor, the next climber is brought up. The second climber removes all the gear placed by the leader while climbing the pitch. When the second climber reaches the stance, the process is repeated until the climb is completed. This form of climbing leaves little evidence, save for some chalk marks, that anyone had ever climbed there; and no gear is (or should be) left behind, except in emergencies.

Sport Climbing: Protection is in the form of bolts placed in the rock at regular intervals, which obviates the need for traditional gear and the technical knowledge needed to use those fiddly camming units and metal wedges. User friendly, with limited risk, it has a greater following than any other form of climbing. Much less experience is required for sport climbing than for traditional climbing. However, the rock is permanently altered by drilling, which poses ethical problems.

Most sport routes are single-pitch climbs 20–30m (66–100ft) long, although there are multipitch routes that are bolted throughout.

Climbs are bolted by the first ascensionist, who checks, cleans and bolts the route. This involves drilling holes into the rock and inserting expansion or glue-in bolts. A hanger is then placed on each bolt to allow for a quickdraw (a short sling) to be attached, through which the rope is passed to protect the leader in the event of a fall. A double-bolt anchor, which can consist of a variety of systems, is also fixed to the rock at the top of the route, or each pitch in the case of a multipitch route, so that the climber can clip in to belay and/or lower off to the ground.

These bolts, hangers and anchors remain in the rock, so all one needs to go sport climbing is a rope and a set of quickdraws, as well as, of course, personal gear such as climbing shoes, harness, chalkbag and belay device.

Right: A climber tests his ability on a short, steep and very 'thin' sport route. Most of the holds on this route are crimps: holds so small that only the very tips of the fingers can be placed on them.

Free Climbing. Contrary to many people's understanding, free climbing does not mean climbing without ropes. It is the act of climbing cleanly on rock using only the rock for hand and foot holds to scale a section of rock; and where the equipment is there only for protection in the event of a fall. As soon as any piece of gear is used for direct aid, like pulling on a sling or standing on a piton, then it becomes aid climbing. Free climbing has a complex (and subjective) grading system that differs from country to country. Generally, the smaller the hand and foot holds, and/or the steeper the route, the more difficult the climbing and the harder the grade.

Aid Climbing. Climbers revert to aid when free climbing becomes too difficult; when holds become too small or disappear completely, or where crack lines become too shallow or narrow to insert a hand or foot. To make further upward progress the climber then has to use equipment placed in the rock for direct aid. This could be one simple move, where pulling on a sling can enable the climber to overcome a blank section to reach good holds again or, at the other extreme, it can entail a mind-bending, death-defying nail-up on a steep, blind seam, relying on specialized aid gear hammered a few millimetres into the rock so that it will sometimes barely take the weight of the climber, let alone the force of a fall. Between these two extremes lie many levels of aid climbing difficulty. Using gear that is not hammered in – cams and nuts – is called clean aiding.

Above: Free solo climbing involves climbing alone and without rope. This climber, 60m (190ft) above the sea, literally holds his life in his hands.

Below left: Aid climbing involves placement of specialized equipment to support a climber's full weight and many extra kilograms of equipment.

Soloing. Most people think of climbing without a rope as soloing. This is correct, but the term refers to anyone climbing alone (without a partner), but not necessarily unroped. Climbing alone and unroped is called free soloing and is only for the strong-minded. This is an uncompromising form of climbing, since any error will almost certainly result in death, but at the same time it is also the most pure, fluent – and often the most rewarding because it is free of the encumbrances of ropes and technical equipment.

Climbing alone and using a rope and gear for protection is called rope soloing. This is less risky than free soloing, but demands experience in the use of equipment and can be very time-consuming, since the climber has to set up self-belay systems and climb every pitch more than once, because he also has to remove the gear placed while climbing.

Big Wall Climbing. There is no defining line where a long route becomes a big wall route, but it invariably means multiple days (and nights) spent out on a rock face of huge proportions. It normally involves a mixture of difficult free and aid climbing. The climbers have to haul hundreds of kilograms of equipment, food, water, warm clothing and portaledges up the route. These routes are often in remote areas like Baffin Island, the Himalayas, or on the storm-ravaged walls of Patagonia. Complicated approaches (often taking days or weeks) and logistical planning can add a more serious dimension to the whole affair. It demands a good understanding of advanced roping techniques and the use of specialized equipment.

Bouldering. This art has been around for a long time, but has only been recognized as a sport in the last 10 years. Climbers string together a series of moves (often of immense difficulty) to create a 'boulder problem'. No ropes or technical equipment are used, or are necessary, because it never takes the climber high off the ground. However, there are exceptions: sometimes climbers push the boat out and get uncomfortably high above the ground. This is known as high-ball bouldering.

Bouldering mats, made of blocks of closed-cell foam covered with a Cordura-type material, are used to cushion falls.

Top: *Overnight bivouacs on the wall are par for the course on big wall climbs. This climber lies ensconced in his sleeping bag on a portaledge far above the ground. Portaledges are designed specifically for this task and come in many different designs. This one is a single-width ledge without tent attachment.*

Above: *Bouldering has become a sport in its own right over the past 10 years.*

INDOOR AND COMPETITION CLIMBING

Indoor climbing. In cities and towns near climbing areas old warehouses, foundries and sometimes churches are transformed into climbing centres. A centre will have a variety of walls, made of various materials (mostly wood), positioned at different angles. Hand and foot holds are placed to design routes of different grades.

Also called 'climbing on plastic', it is popular with climbers from the entire spectrum of the sport. Some use these centres for training work-outs to increase their power, endurance and technique. Others use it during the week to keep up their fitness between weekend climbing trips. And some just go there to have fun. Indeed, nowadays there are many people who only climb on plastic and never venture outdoors onto real rock. It has become an important aspect of the sport.

Competition climbing. The first climbing competition took place in the village of Arco in Italy in the early 1980s. It was held on a rock face where artificial holds had been chipped into the rock to design routes of increasing difficulty. Climbers were eliminated in each round. Changing the rock in this way had huge repercussions and today climbing competitions, bar a few exceptions, are held indoors. This allows for precise route setting and designing different walls for every competition. Hundreds of

Above: *Competitor in action on 'Impending Wall' at The Foundary, Sheffield, in the United Kingdom.*

competitions take place around the globe every year. There are a few invitation-only events for the elite climbers and there is also the World Cup circuit. These are all 'difficulty' competitions, where competitors' high points determine whether they go through to the next round. Conversely, the routes in speed climbing competitions are not very difficult and climbers race each other up identical routes. Bouldering competitions have become popular not only because of the sport's massive following, but also because it is much cheaper to stage than the more standard, indoor, competition. Bouldering competitions are usually held outdoors at a recognized bouldering area where a number of pre-set 'problems' are climbed. Points are allocated to each problem, with the person accumulating the most points at the end of the day declared the winner.

Above: *Climbing a typical, low-angled, frozen watercourse. The climber is using rigid crampons for greater stability on thin water ice and mixed ground. Also note the rock protection used where the rock is exposed, since ice gear is useless on such thin ice.*

ICE CLIMBING

The term ice climbing covers a number of activities where a climber will use crampons and ice axes over a section of ice, using ice screws for protection, but also traditional rock gear where exposed rock can be found amid the ice. It can involve low-angled ice fields or impressive iced-up couloirs; rock faces covered in verglas; or frozen waterfalls forming huge columns of ice, from thick fluted pillars to slender, fragile ribbons of ice.

Ice climbing is done in a winter environment and therefore often wears a more serious cloak than rock climbing. Besides the more extreme weather, the medium of ice will always change from one season to the next, posing a different problem every time (sometimes easier, sometimes more difficult), as opposed to rock climbs, which remain the same year in, year out.

DRY TOOLING

This is a hybrid of ice climbing and rock climbing done mostly on rock with ice-climbing equipment. The climber will use specially modified crampons and axes to climb overhanging sections of rock. The points of axes and crampons are used to find small cracks and crevices in the rock to facilitate upward movement. This form of climbing is frequently bolt-protected, because the nature of the climbing is so extreme that traditional protection is impossible.

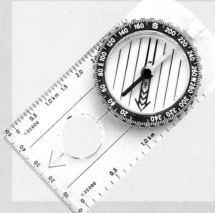

ROCK TYPES AND TERRAIN

One of my greatest passions in life is to travel to different parts of the world to discover and experience different mountains and diverse climbing areas. No crag is the same and no crack, hand hold or foot hold has a twin anywhere on the planet. This is what I love about climbing. No climb or move can be compared with another; every route is unique and has its own individual character. And to make matters more interesting our planet has been adorned with many different rock types and also variations of the same rock type from country to country.

Rock types

Most of the world's climbing takes place on three main rock types: granite, limestone and sandstone. Within each group, there is enormous variety. The granite on the mighty walls and domes of Yosemite Valley in California is fine grained (and probably offers the best granite climbing anywhere) and very different from the granite found in the European Alps. And both are totally different to the rougher and more friable granite of Namibia's desert domes. These differences are mainly due to the age of the rock, the circumstances under which it was formed and the erosion and weather conditions it has been subjected to over millions of years.

Different rock types also offer different styles of climbing. For instance, **granite** offers mainly long crack systems, wafer type flakes (due to exfoliation) and sweeping slabs often adorned with little quartz knobs that require some getting used to, as it demands good balance and confidence in using tiny foot grips.

Sandstone is generally steeper, with many vertical cracks and horizontal rails (breaks). It accepts protection gear quite easily, although in a few places such as East Germany it can be too soft to accept protection. Sandstone is also well known for its overhangs, some of them quite substantial.

Limestone is also variable, but it is generally compact, offering few options for placing natural protection.

For this reason traditional climbing on limestone can often be very runout (long distances between protection) and therefore scary and mentally taxing.

The limestone crags that enrich the countryside of Italy, France, Spain and other European countries, and Asian countries such as Thailand, offer some of the best sport climbing in the world – routes that wouldn't exist under the banner of traditional climbing, due to the compact nature and sheerness of the rock.

When venturing onto a new crag of a different rock type or a style of climbing that you are not used to, be cautious. Drop a few grades. Do some easy routes until you come to grips with the technique required to climb this rock. Then, when you feel more comfortable, start pushing the boat out.

If you have sharpened your claws on steep, hard sandstone that offers good solid grips and excellent protection, you will feel way out of your depth when you first step onto a steep granite slab that

Top right: A climber ascends a typical flake on the fine-grained granite high in the French Alps.
Centre right: The Humanality route takes a spectacular line up the middle of this limestone wall on Tonsai Beach in Thailand.
Bottom right: A climber pulls into a steep corner using rails and cracks typical of the red sandstone in the Cederberg mountains of South Africa.

requires good friction technique and a fine sense of balance. The same applies the other way round. All it takes is a little time and patience to learn a different set of rules and you can be on your way.

If you look at rock types around the world, it seems that the northern hemisphere has a plethora of excellent limestone crags, while most of the good sandstone climbing lies in the southern hemisphere. Australia's Blue Mountains and Arapiles have some of the best sandstone climbing in the world, so also have the Cederberg mountains of South Africa.

There are also some unique rock types scattered around the world: England's gritstone edges, for instance. This rock has a rough texture, but most of the holds and rails are rounded and it is often difficult to find protection.

Volcanic rock such as rhyolite gives varied and interesting climbing on often pocketed walls, while slate has a totally different feel, being smooth with thin cracks and tiny, sharp edges.

One thing is certain: no matter where in the world you are, or on whatever rock you are climbing, there will always be times when you have to deal with friable, brittle, or unsound rock. Climbing on bad rock can be very unnerving and demands experience and a cool head. You need to spread your weight evenly. Don't pull too hard with or stand too hard on any one limb. Check to see in which

direction it would be best to use certain holds. An outward pull is often not recommended on suspect blocks or fragile flakes, but on the same holds a downward pull could be relatively safe.

A few years back, while climbing in the Dolomites, I complained to an Italian climber about the poor quality of the rock. 'You can't pull on anything' I said. 'No, no my friend' he replied. 'In the Dolomites you don't pull the rock, you push against it.'

Test any hold that looks even slightly suspect. Give it a good kick, or a solid thunk with the heel of your hand. The sound will generally tell you what you need to know. A hollow dull sound means that the piece of rock is not fully part of the surrounding wall and needs to be treated with care.

Weather

When venturing out on the mountains, whether it is to climb on a small crag a short walk from your car, a day trip into the hills, or an expedition to one of the great ranges in the world, your first concern is always the weather and how it will affect your plans. Even though you may plan a trip to coincide with the best expected weather for the area, weather is a fickle beast and can change its mind at the flash of a lightning bolt. There are never any guarantees, and the bigger the mountains, the less chance of stable conditions for lengthy periods.

Some areas are notorious for bad weather. A Scottish climber once told me: 'If it's not raining in Scotland, just wait a little while.' Patagonia, with its committing

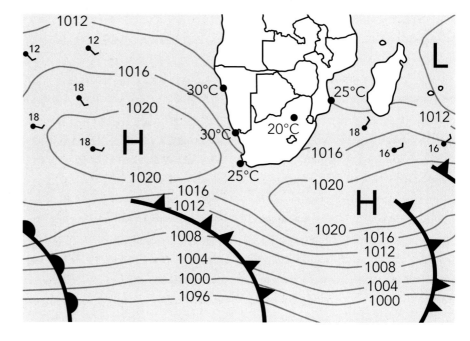

walls, is also respected for its stormy weather and strong winds.

Meteorological weather forecasts are very accurate these days and should always be checked before setting out. However, many forecasts are given for the surrounding towns and the weather can be much harsher 1000m (3300ft) higher. For example, whereas the forecast for a town nestled at the foot of high mountains may be partly cloudy, it would probably be raining, or worse, at a higher elevation. It is up to you to decide what the differences will be and go equipped for those eventualities. Remember that the higher you go, the more the temperature drops. As a general rule on a clear day the temperature will drop by 1°C (2.12°F) for every 100m (330ft) of height gained. Wind can also have an effect on the temperature. Strong winds with low temperatures can be a deadly mixture.

Weather prediction is a blend of science and art. You need a good meteorological forecast, some reliable local information and common sense.

Left: *A synoptic chart supplies information about cold fronts, wind direction and speed, rainfall, temperatures, etc. The circular lines are isobars that link all areas with the same air pressure. These are arranged around high or low pressure areas. Lines with triangles represent cold fronts and lines with semicircles represent warm fronts.*

Cirrostratus (mares' tails): thin wisps of cloud, or ice crystals, often occurring at the high edge of a warm front.

Cirrocumulus: globular masses of ice crystals at high altitude; indicating changing conditions.

Cirrus: wispy clouds that can indicate a warm front approaching.

Cumulonimbus: these enormous cumulus clouds are a forewarning of thunder and hailstorms, and heavy, unpredictable winds.

Altostratus: blueish-grey layers of cloud which blot out the sky; they precede drizzle, rain or snow.

Altocumulus: large globular cumulus clouds at high altitude; when dark grey, rainfall may occur.

Nimbostratus: thick, dark, grey layer across sky; ice crystals in upper level. Brings continuous rain or snow.

Stratocumulus: tight cumulus layers; showers are possible.

Cumulus: 'cotton puff' formations, usually occurring when the weather is fine. Dark cumulus clouds bring showers.

Stratus: low-occurring layered cloud; can indicate a warm front approaching, with light rain. A darker, thicker, wetter version of this is known as Nimbostratus.

WHAT TO LOOK OUT FOR

When planning a trip, find out as much as you can about the weather patterns that affect the area where you want to climb. Speak to local climbers. The kind of questions you should ask are:

- From which direction does the bad weather approach?
- What are the prevailing winds and which are the ones that you need to worry about?
- Are there any dominant weather patterns, like late afternoon storms?
- What cloud formations are the forerunners of bad weather? Is it the high, streaky cirrus clouds? Or those evil-looking fish-shaped clouds that call for an instant retreat on the committing walls of Patagonia?

HYPOTHERMIA: SYMPTOMS, TREATMENT AND PREVENTION

Hypothermia results when the body temperature drops too far below the optimum body temperature of 36.9°C (98.4°F) and the functions of the body become impaired.

Symptoms: Shivering, stumbling, confusion, slow speech and the refusal of assistance are early warning signs. If left untreated the next stage is characterized by the inability to walk or stand, irrationality and disorientation – when the patient can start to strip away clothing and sleeping bags. From semi-consciousness, the patient slips into unconsciousness with a very weak heartbeat. Finally the heart and breathing stop.

Treatment: Get the patient out of the cold and rain. Change into dry, warm clothing and administer warm fluids. Generate heat in the shelter with a candle or stove. The body can be heated externally by doubling up in a sleeping bag with a second person for additional body heat.

When rewarming the patient, it is essential that the process is started on the central core of the body and not the extremities. Warming the extremities first will encourage the cold blood in the extremities to flow towards the core. Never give alcohol, because this dilates the blood vessels and results in loss of heat.

Prevention: This condition can be prevented by having the correct equipment: warm, waterproof, windproof clothing, and consuming adequate food and liquid. A wet person in cold wind is asking for trouble. A bivvy, survival bag or 'Bothy' can be a real life-saver, particularly in cold, wet, UK-type conditions.

Above: This climber is high in the mountains and bad weather is brewing. This is a dangerous situation and it would be prudent to seek shelter as soon as possible.

EXTREME WEATHER

If you climb for long enough you will sooner or later have to deal with bad weather conditions.

Getting caught out on a long multipitch climb, or high on an Alpine peak in adverse weather can be unpleasant, dangerous and quite character building.

Prolonged exposure to low temperatures, particularly at high altitudes, can quickly lead to frostbite. Toes and fingers are normally the first to be affected. Ears and noses suffer too.

Hypothermia is a life-threatening drop in the body's core temperature (see above).

Another terrifying scenario is being caught out on a high peak, or exposed wall during an electric storm with nowhere to hide. Climbers have been killed by lightning strikes. Having loads of metal climbing equipment slung around your person doesn't help matters and it is best, under these conditions, to stash your gear some distance away to avoid attracting lightning.

When the great Italian alpinist, Walter Bonatti, and six other climbers were caught in an electric storm high on the Central Pillar of Freney on Mont Blanc, they tried to sit out the storm. They spent several days in freezing conditions, getting totally soaked and dodging lightning bolts, before realizing that retreat was the only way out. Four of the seven died before they reached the safety of the closest mountain hut. All four deaths were due to a mixture of exhaustion and hypothermia.

A beautiful, hot day can also have devastating consequences for the unprepared, especially at higher altitudes, where the atmosphere allows greater radiation from the sun. Sunburn, dehydration and heat stroke are very common and precautions should be taken (see hyperthermia p26).

Regardless of the weather forecast, or how good the weather looks when you set off on your

---

FROSTNIP AND FROSTBITE: SYMPTOMS, TREATMENT AND PREVENTION

When a climber is exposed to sub-zero temperatures, especially in windy conditions and at high altitude, the extremities of the body can develop frostnip which, left untreated, will advance to frostbite, when ice crystals form in the tissue, damaging or destroying it. The body tries to protect its core temperature by diverting the blood supply from the extremities to the core. Frostnip and frostbite commonly occur in the toes, fingers and the tips of the nose and ears.

FROSTNIP

Symptoms: The skin turns white; affected areas go numb and are no longer painful.

Treatment: If spotted early enough, frostnip can be treated quite successfully in the field. Warm the affected areas by applying body heat (preferably someone else's), like stuffing the toes into the groin area, or in the armpits. Fingers can be warmed by placing them in the mouth. If feeling does not return within an hour or so, then the condition should be treated as frostbite.

FROSTBITE

This is a much more serious condition and develops if frostnip is not treated timeously. The cells making up the tissue actually freeze, with a high risk of permanent tissue loss. Frostbite occurs on two levels: superficial (nerve damage, but no tissue loss) and deep (tissue loss due to the onset of gangrene).

Symptoms: Early signs include waxy, hard skin. All feeling of cold and pain disappear. Area later becomes black and blistered.

Treatment: Find shelter immediately. The affected area should not be rubbed or massaged. The person should be warmed through extra clothing and blankets. Direct heat should never be applied. Frostbite cannot be solely treated in the field. Basic treatment is similar to frostnip, but then the patient should be evacuated to professional medical care to prevent loss of digits. Blistered skin should be covered with a dressing and left unburst. Thawed tissue should never be allowed to refreeze.

Prevention: Keep warm by wearing the correct clothing. Wear good, insulated and waterproof boots and gloves and always try to stay as dry as possible. Wiggling, beating and stomping can help circulation.

HYPERTHERMIA: SYMPTOMS, TREATMENT AND PREVENTION

The body becomes overheated through exercise, overinsulation, exposure to heat and inadequate fluid intake. Heatstroke develops when the body's ability to cool itself by sweating fails. The onset can be sudden and, untreated, it can result in collapse and death. The body cools itself down by the evaporation of perspiration on the skin. If a person becomes severely dehydrated, perspiration may stop, thereby robbing the body of its natural cooling system. Under humid conditions, the cooling effect of evaporation will be impaired.

Symptoms: Rapid pulse, rapid shallow breathing, headache, loss of appetite, nausea, weakness and dizziness. At first (heat exhaustion) the skin will be cold and clammy. Once heatstroke sets in the skin will be dry and flushed. The patient will be hot to the touch; may become confused, disorientated and refuse help. Seizures are possible.

Treatment: Get the patient to a cool place out of the sun. Cool by giving the patient cool water to drink, applying cool, wet cloths against the skin and fanning. Dehydration can cause shock, because the blood volume is reduced, so you should get the person to lie down and raise the feet about 30cm (12 in) higher than the head.

Prevention:
- Drink lots of liquid. A good gauge of dehydration is the frequency and colour of your urine. Frequent, clear urine is a good sign.
- Wear loose-fitting light-coloured clothing.
- Wear a wide-brimmed hat and wet it at river crossings. This aids the cooling process.
- Wear sun-block cream.
- Rest in shady spots at regular intervals and take advantage of a cool swim on hot days.

climb, it is foolhardy not to take at least a warm fleece and a waterproof top and trousers. If there is a possibility of really cold conditions, then add gloves, a balaclava, maybe even a down jacket.

A cellphone (mobile), if there is coverage, could make the difference when a life is at stake.

WHAT TO DO WHEN YOU'RE CAUGHT IN BAD WEATHER

There are no hard-and-fast rules. It depends on many factors. How bad is the weather really? What is your position? What extreme weather clothing and equipment do you have between you? The general rule is to stay put and sit the weather out, but, of course, there will be exceptions. If some members of the group are not adequately clothed, then sitting out a storm could mean almost certain death for them. It is never an easy call in the face of extreme weather, but the leader must decide on the safest course of action and then act decisively and confidently. If possible, contact rescue services, even if only for stand-by purposes, so that they will be able to act immediately when needed.

Navigation

Finding the start of the climb, working out where it goes and climbing the route, is often only half the adventure. The other half is getting off the mountain and back to the safety of your car or mountain hut. Descents can be long, complex journeys that demand good mountain sense and sound navigational skills. You also need good observation skills, especially if you are returning in the direction from which you came. Navigation starts when you shut the car door. Some routes do not have a path leading up to the start of the climb. You need to prepare before you set off by asking climbers who have done the route recently; reading guide books; and asking local guides. And don't forget to ask about the descent route.

If you are crossing a mountain range, or even a single mountain that covers a large area, especially in poor visibility, then a map, compass and altimeter are essential equipment.

MAP READING

All maps are originally created in such a way that the top of the page will point towards the North Pole, although this is not always how they are published. A compass rose on the map will indicate where north is. The map is made up of a series of lines, symbols, shaded areas and names, with a key to the symbols.

The contour lines indicate the altitude at any given point and, on most mountaineering maps, will be drawn in at 20m (65ft) intervals, or 10m (33ft) in Great Britain. The closer they are together, the steeper the gradient.

Some modern maps also use colour to show at a glance where the low lying areas and the higher plateaux are, or where the snowline begins. Roads, rivers, boundaries and foot paths are also marked. Maps can also indicate places of historical and contemporary interest, bodies of water, towns, parking areas on mountain passes and plantations. Ideally, a map should be an exact, scaled-down replica of the land.

Scale A map designed for mountaineering purposes typically has a scale of 1:50 000. This means that one unit of measurement on the map is equivalent to 50,000 on the ground. In other words, 2cm on the map equals 1km on the ground (2 inches on the map equals 1.58 miles on the ground).

Contours are lines on a map which join up areas of equal altitude and are set at intervals to dictate the shape and height of the land. The closer the lines are to each other, the steeper the terrain.

Gridlines are drawn in a north-south and east-west direction and on a 1:50 000 map, for example, they are normally set at intervals of between 1km (0.62 mile) and 5km (3 miles). These lines help with setting your compass to the map for a bearing; estimating distances; and identifying your position on the map in terms of collective reference points within a given grid square. Not all nations' maps have a grid – some use latitude and longitude. A few have neither!

Contours and shapes

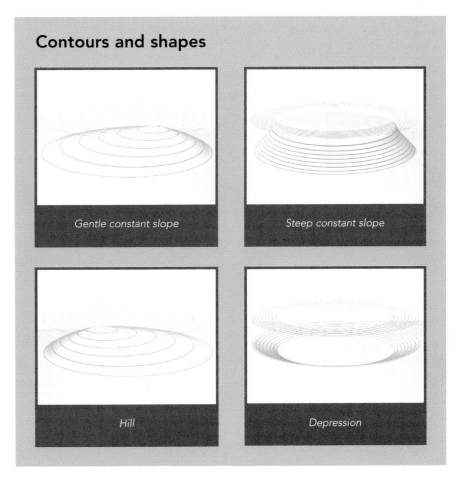

Gentle constant slope

Steep constant slope

Hill

Depression

Above: *Contours and shapes that are used on a typical map.*

THE COMPASS

A compass has a floating, swivelling needle which should always point to magnetic north. It also has a protractor, orienting lines, a measuring scale and a base plate on which everything is mounted.

Magnetic north, where compass needles point from virtually every place on the planet, is currently 966km (600 miles) from geographic north, or the North Terrestrial pole, the fixed point that marks the axis of the turning planet. The angle between magnetic north (somewhere in north-east Canada) and geographic north can vary considerably from place to place, and this variation is indicated on all good maps (see 'Poles Apart'). To navigate accurately across mountainous terrain, you need to get the map and the compass working together.

Study the map and determine your current position and your destination. Examine the area between the two. You may be able to walk in a relatively straight line, but often this will be impossible due to gorges, or buttresses in your direct path. In this case you need to work out a route skirting these obstacles.

If visibility is poor, then compass bearings become important to help you keep direction.

GLOBAL POSITIONING SYSTEM (GPS)

A handheld GPS can now be carried by climbers and hikers. It works off satellite readings and can pinpoint your position anywhere on the planet to within a few metres; map out your route; read your elevation above sea level; check your speed and save waypoints of any features to which you

need to return. Together with sound map-reading skills a GPS can be invaluable.

POLES APART

The North Magnetic Pole is distinct from the North Terrestrial Pole, the fixed point that marks the axis of the turning planet. The magnetic pole is currently 966 kilometres (600 miles) from the geographic one.

The North Magnetic Pole acts somewhat like a giant magnet and is the location to which compasses point from virtually every place on the planet.

The earth's magnetic field originates in the outer core, produced by the movement of molten iron more than 3000km (1850 miles) below the surface and influenced to some degree by charged particles streaming from the sun.

Updated charts that delineate the North Magnetic Pole's current location are necessary to plot accurate courses for navigation. The erratic pole can jump around considerably each day, but migrates about 10–40km (6–25 miles) each year. It is resurveyed at least once every decade and the new data made available to map publishers.

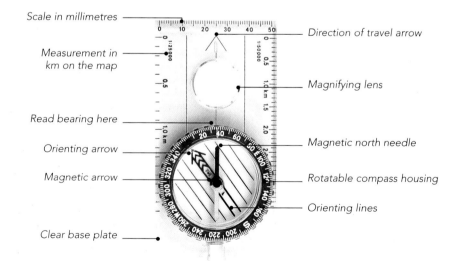

Scale in millimetres — Direction of travel arrow
Measurement in km on the map — Magnifying lens
Read bearing here — Magnetic north needle
Orienting arrow — Rotatable compass housing
Magnetic arrow — Orienting lines
Clear base plate

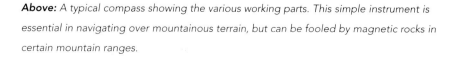

Above: *A typical compass showing the various working parts. This simple instrument is essential in navigating over mountainous terrain, but can be fooled by magnetic rocks in certain mountain ranges.*

THE ALTIMETER

An altimeter measures the air pressure, from which it can calculate the altitude. The problem with pressure-based altimeters is that its reading is affected by changing weather, which is accompanied by a change in air pressure, thus giving a false altitude reading. To reduce the possibility of a false reading you should reset your altimeter at all known altitude points – when you reach a landmark, or beacon that you can identify on the map, and which either gives an altitude or from which you can calculate an altitude on the map.

The altimeter can be invaluable in bad visibility or when you need to change direction on steep ground at a certain altitude; or know when you have reached the crest of a ridge. Non-pressure-based altimeters, which work off satellite readings, are available. They are more expensive, also more accurate, but won't work as a barometer.

NAVIGATIONAL FLAIR

Even with all the tools of the trade, navigation needs some personal flair to make everything fall into place. Use common sense. Don't blunder off blindly on your bearing. First look at the variables: estimate the time it will take to get from point A to point B, taking into consideration the gradient and the roughness of the terrain to be covered. Memorize the landmarks you are likely to encounter between the two points, like a river crossing, the crest of a ridge, a ravine, or even a road. This will provide reassurance and keep you on the right track. Rather over-estimate the time it will take and never try to force the terrain to match the map, in the conviction that you are in the right place. Remember, any mistake made in navigation can only be compounded the further you travel before rectifying it.

Distance travelled can be estimated by using Naismith's Rule. Naismith was a Scottish hiker who calculated that he could walk at 5km per hour (3 miles per hour) over flat terrain. Then he would add 30 minutes for every 300m (1000ft) of altitude gained. With a bit of adjustment you can work out your own rate of travel.

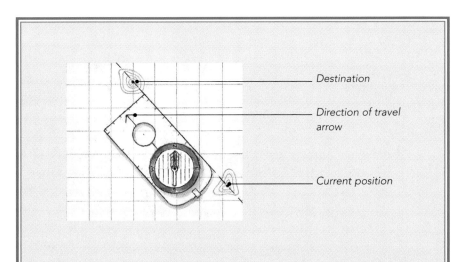

Destination

Direction of travel arrow

Current position

Your given information is your present position and destination point. Place one long edge of the compass plate along the line joining these two points, making sure that the 'direction-of-travel-arrow' is pointing in the direction of intended travel and not back towards you. Then swivel the compass housing until the parallel lines drawn on the base of the compass housing run parallel with the vertical edge of the map, in line with the north-south grid lines on the map. This should line up the orienting arrow with the north arrow on the map. You now have a bearing that must be adjusted to the magnetic variation. The angle of magnetic variation should be printed on the map and will vary, depending on where you are in the world. The variation is dialled on to the compass housing. Once you have made this adjustment you can apply your bearing to the ground.

Access and the environment

By the very nature of the sport, climbing takes us to some of the most beautiful places on earth: from limestone towers bursting straight from the sea in Thailand to sweeping granite walls of America's Yosemite Valley to the majestic mountains of the Himalaya. There are many more of course, but one thing is cast in stone: wherever the human race has set foot will never be the same again.

A prime example is Railay Beach in Thailand – a climber's paradise that has become an environmentalist's nightmare. The peninsula, once covered in virgin jungle, has over the years become a scarred and built-up eyesore. Obviously the Thai people saw the economic potential in attracting climbers to the area and started the process of building and excavating. Every season more trees are ripped out and more bungalows built.

In many parts of the world, areas of extraordinary beauty are declared national parks, wilderness areas and reserves.

Many climbing areas fall within the boundaries of these parks, often making access difficult, impossible, or very expensive. Today, access is an important consideration and there are organizations that deal with issues arising from it. The majority of climbers are staunch environmentalists who know that access to a climbing area is a privilege. Unfortunately, one careless action by a thoughtless individual, such as parking in front of a gate, or leaving a cigarette butt at the base of a crag, will often suffice to prompt a ranger or farmer to deny climbers access to the area in future. Climbers the world over will always have to negotiate with land owners and government agencies to be allowed to climb on the mountains that essentially belong to everyone.

Above: *Paine National Park, one of the world's great unspoilt mountain sanctuaries. However, constant use by mountaineers and trekkers will have an impact over time.*

Ice and snow

A rock climb remains constant. Every move is exactly the same as when you last did the route 20 years ago and the crux sequence is cast in stone – literally!

With snow and ice, routes change from season to season. Some seasons there are routes that, due to weather conditions, don't form at all. There are famous ice routes, such as the *Diamond Couloir* on Mount Kenya, that will probably never form again due to global warming.

Ice and snow is an unpredictable medium. Climbing on snow and ice would not be possible without tools such as crampons, ice axes, and various protection gear like ice screws and dead boy belays. But even with all the right gear, venturing out onto frozen terrain can involve dealing with many objective hazards.

Technical ability is, however, secondary to the depth of a climber's knowledge and experience of the phenomena of avalanches, safe travel over glaciers and through ice-falls, mountain weather, the hazards of falling rocks and toppling seracs, collapsing cornices and the signs of altitude sickness.

An alpine climber should be able to look at conditions on any given route or mountain and be able to judge whether the route would be reasonably safe to climb or not.

Most alpine routes cover mixed ground and the climber is likely to encounter different snow and ice features along the way.

When climbing on mixed ground or on frozen waterfalls, the condition of the snow or ice is a critical factor concerning the safety of the route. These conditions can be greatly affected by the time of day. For instance, ice couloirs should always be climbed or crossed in the frozen temperatures

Above: *The extremely popular climbing area of Railay Beach in Thailand showing evidence of massive deforestation driven by the need to build more bungalows to accommodate tourists.*

of darkness. As soon as the sun touches the top of a couloir, the snow will start melting, thereby releasing a volley of rocks and debris down the couloir, turning it into a death trap. This also goes for any sort of travel beneath steep, iced-up chutes or walls.

A good example is the notorious North Wall of the Eiger. It is near suicidal to be caught out on the icefields in the middle of the day: the sun melts the top sections of the wall, and tons of debris are funnelled down the White Spider, directly above the Second Icefield.

That is why it is common to start an Alpine route at 01:00 or 02:00. At this hour of the day the conditions are perfect, rendering the snow crisp and frozen.

COMMON FEATURES ON A STANDARD ALPINE ROUTE

Moraine: This is a jumble of boulders and old ice normally found at the foot of a glacier.

Glacier: You often need to cross or ascend a glacier to get to the start of a route. Glaciers are basically frozen rivers and, like rivers, they move – some faster than others, depending on the steepness of the terrain. Because of this continuous motion, cracks and crevasses form, move and disappear.

Seracs: These are ice towers that are formed when glaciers become very steep and the ice breaks up. Areas where they are continually forming and falling are known as icefalls. Seracs can also be formed when ice cliffs break up.

Couloirs: These are simply gullies that have become iced up. They can be used as access to a route, but solidly iced-up couloirs often form good ice routes themselves.

Verglas: When a cold snap follows a thaw, a thin layer of frozen ice develops over rocks. The ice is too thin for ice tools to gain purchase.

Bergschrund: Where a glacier or ice field meets a rock wall, the ice tends to recede, causing a chasm to form between the rock and the ice.

Cornice: These are formed by the wind blowing across the top of a ridge, sculpting the snow into a curved plume. The windward side is smooth and rounded, while on the opposite side an overhang of unstable snow is formed, which can break under a climber's weight.

Above: On the Eiger North Face. Eric Jones solos across the Third Ice Field, which leads to The Ramp and the upper section of the 'Eiger Wand' 1938 Route.

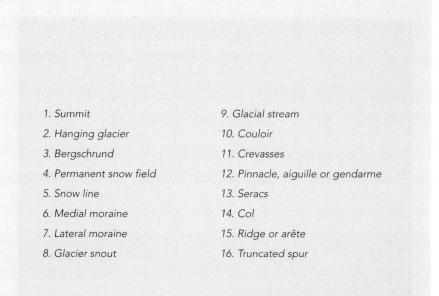

1. Summit
2. Hanging glacier
3. Bergschrund
4. Permanent snow field
5. Snow line
6. Medial moraine
7. Lateral moraine
8. Glacier snout
9. Glacial stream
10. Couloir
11. Crevasses
12. Pinnacle, aiguille or gendarme
13. Seracs
14. Col
15. Ridge or arête
16. Truncated spur

Above: *Climbers should familiarize themselves with the different features of an alpine mountainscape; how they are formed and how the weather affects them.*

Grading

Grading is like language: almost every country has its own and you don't really understand how it works until you have climbed in that country quite frequently. It is also very subjective: a climber who excels at crack climbing will consider a particular crack much easier than most others. Who gives the correct grading to that?

One of the first grading systems to be invented was the British one. Still in use today, it is one of the most accurate (although at first glance it looks quite complicated). It ranges from 'easy' at the bottom of the scale, through 'moderate', 'difficult', 'severe to 'extremely severe'. During the 1960s the top grade was XS (extremely severe) and any climb harder than HVS (hard very severe) was given the XS grade. Soon there were too many climbs of varying grades being stuffed into the XS category, so XS was divided into E grades, from E1 to E10 (E standing for extreme).

This system was devised to give the overall grade of the route, but then a technical grade was still needed to denote the hardest move on a particular pitch. So another grading system was devised for this purpose: one that used numbers subdivided by a, b and c, for example E2 5c.

In the 1930s the Americans adopted the European grading system, which simply ran from class 1 to class 6, with classes 1 to 3 representing trail walking to simple scrambling; class 4 more challenging scrambling, but without the need for ropes; class 5 free climbing of a more serious nature; and class 6 aid climbing. However, free climbing spanned a wide range of difficulty in one grade.

In the early 1950s legendary climbers Royal Robbins and Don Wilson modified the system. They decided to subdivide class 5, with 5.9 reserved for the hardest stuff of the day. This system later became known as the Yosemite Decimal System and is still in use, although it has been extended to keep up with the ever-evolving nature of rock climbing (see chart).

Other countries devised their own systems. Some of these are rough-and-ready, while others are extremely sensitive. Grading will always be hotly debated.

South Africa	Australia	France	USA	U.K.	UIAA Germany
9	9	3	5.4	diff	III
10	10	3+	5.5	V. diff	III +
11	11	4-	5.6	Mild S	IV
12	12	4	5.6	Severe	IV+
13	12	4	5.7	Hard S	IV+
14	13	4+	5.8	Hard S	V-
15	14	5a	5.8	VS	V
16	15	5b	5.9	VS	V
17	16	5c	5.9	HVS	V+
18	16	6a	5.10a	HVS	VI-
19	17	6a	5.10b	E1	VI
20	18	6a+	5.10c	E2	VI+
21	19	6b	5.10d	E2/3	VII-
22	20	6b+	5.11a	E3	VII
23	21	6c	5.11b	E4	VII+
24	22/23	6c+	5.11c	E4/5	VII+
25	24	7a	5.11d/12a	E5	VIII-
26	25	7a+	5.12a/b	E5/6	VIII
27	26	7b	5.12b/c	E5/6	VIII+
28	27	7b+/7c	5.12c/d	E6	IX-
29	28	7c+	5.13a	E6/7	IX
30	28/29	8a	5.13b	E7	IX+
31	30	8a+	5.13c/d	E7	X-
32	31	8b	5.14a	E8	X
33	32/33	8b+	5.14a/b	E8	X
34	34	8c	5.14b	E9	X+
35	35	8c+	5.14c	E10	XI-
36	36	9a	5.14d	E10/11	XI

Ethics

Our behaviour in the mountains and on the crags is governed by a set of unwritten rules. However, ethical differences have been around from the beginning. For instance, who has the rightful claim to the first ascent of a route? How ethical was the behaviour of Edward Whymper when he snatched victory from Antoine Carrel in making the first ascent of the famed Matterhorn — and hurled rocks down at the defeated party from the summit?

Over the years certain understandings have been reached that protect the rights of climbers, but, again, these are only as ethical as the person wielding the axe.

For example, an average climber may make the first ascent of an impressive wall, using bolts drilled into the rock to scale the harder sections. This is done often and is generally accepted. However, the following year a better climber, who doesn't need the bolts, makes the second ascent of the route. He chops the bolts and carries on to make a 'clean' free ascent. Was it ethical to remove the bolts?

Another example is that of someone opening a traditional route on a dedicated sport (bolted) crag, a crag to which no one will bring traditional equipment. According to an unwritten law of climbing, the first 'ascensionist' must consent to the route being bolted, otherwise it stays a traditional route. So here is a route that could remain unclimbed due to an ethical conundrum.

The French were the leading exponents of bolted climbing when it became fashionable about 20 years ago. They would abseil (rappel) down a potential line, inspect it, clean it, work the moves on top rope, then bolt the route from top down and eventually lead the climb in red point style (see glossary). Doing routes in this style was totally unacceptable to climbers in other countries. However, the French started climbing much harder grades and were soon considered the best climbing nation. It took the rest of the world some years to accept bolting top down. However, some climbers still have strong views on this, and on bolting a route that could be climbed with traditional gear.

On the other extreme are the Himalayan expeditions. These days fast alpine, oxygenless ascents of the giant 8000m (26,000ft) peaks by super-athletic climbers are common. How ethical is it to ascend by the old methods with hoards of porters laying siege on a mountain, slowly making your way up via a string of camps, sucking supplementary oxygen?

These are just some of the ethical questions that occupy the minds of climbers and become the subject of fireside conversations.

First route used by the party to ascend in order to reach the top anchors of the route from which they wish to top-rope

Bolted route

Route being climbed

Above: *People sometimes use an easy route to access a harder route, which they then top-rope. In this case the climber had ascended by the left hand route, traversed to a route on the right, crossing a bolted route in the middle, thus hogging three routes. Only one of the three routes on this wall can be climbed now.*

EQUIPMENT AND GEAR

This sport is very equipment reliant and climbing traditional routes, especially, requires a great deal of expensive equipment. However, if you are just starting out, you will probably be accompanied by a more experienced climber, who already has all the paraphernalia. In this case there is no need to break the bank to get all that equipment, although you will need your own personal gear.

Above: A collection of climbing gear needed for a day at the crag: Rope, harness, climbing shoes, belay devices, quickdraws, helmet. This is essential equipment to ensure safety and enjoyment when climbing.

The basics

Climbing shoes: Without these you will have little confidence in (or chance of) your feet staying on small foot holds. There are hundreds of different brands, each offering a variety of cuts and styles. If this is your first pair, you should go for comfort rather than too tight a fit, although they must be nothing less than snug. Also, stay away from the expensive, sporty looking models, since these are designed for experienced climbers with good footwork. A pair of these on your feet will last a few months, perhaps, before the lining starts coming through the rand. Get a cheaper pair with thick rubber and a stiffish sole. This should last you through your apprenticeship, after which, if you are still as keen as a bean, you can buy one of the racy models.

Harness: A harness, on anyone's butt, can last in excess of five years. The main reason for buying a new harness, is not because your old one is worn out, but that you want to upgrade to the latest model.

Since you don't have to start with a cheap one, I suggest you go for a padded, fully adjustable harness that will fit when you are in your skimpy sport climbing outfit and also when wearing thick fleece while trad climbing.

Test the harness. Most stores have a point from which you can hang. Sit in the harness and make sure it is comfortable before parting with your money.

Chalk bag: Inexpensive, it can last indefinitely and is essential for serious climbing. First find one into which you can get your hand comfortably and then choose one that looks cool.

Belay device: Your belay device (with locking karabiner) should always be clipped to your harness, whether you are wearing it or carrying it in your rucksack.

There are many different types, all doing the same job: locking the rope in the event of a fall. All belay devices also double up as abseil devices. Make sure to get a decent-sized locking karabiner to go with it.

Clothing

If you are going out to a crag for a day of singlepitch fun, then a mid-thigh length, loosefitting pair of shorts or, if it is cold, trousers, and a T-shirt or tank top will suffice. Even if it is a beautiful warm day, however, always throw a fleece top and at least a decent windbreaker in your rucksack, in case the weather changes. If the wind picks up on a shady crag, it can become rather chilly around the gills.

When planning a multipitch route in mountains further afield, you need to be a bit more specific about clothing, especially if it has to be carried up the route in a rucksack. Weather will play an important role, but regardless of the forecast, you should always go out into the mountains prepared for bad weather. Clothing for alpine climbing, extreme big wall and Himalayan expeditions will be covered in later chapters.

For climbing in the local hills, you can choose from:

- A polypropylene shirt (short or long sleeved) to be worn against the skin. These garments wick sweat away from the body, always keeping the skin dry and therefore warmer.
- A thin polartec fleece top (for slightly chilly conditions).
- A thicker polartec top (for colder conditions), preferably with wind stop properties.
- A breathable waterproof top is essential. Choose something lightweight.
- A pair of trousers made of a light stretch polartec is comfortable in hot and cool conditions.
- Gloves are optional, but handy when belaying on cold, windy stances (see glossary).
- A pair of approach shoes that are lightweight for carrying up the rock climb to be worn again for the descent.

Below: Regardless of what the weather looks like, you should always be prepared for cold weather. Not only does mountain weather change suddenly, but keeping warm on blustery afternoons will make the day more enjoyable.

Special gear for trad and sport climbing

Wouldn't it wonderful if we could shed all the ropes and hardware to climb with shoes and a chalk bag only? However, unless you can be guaranteed never to fall, you need lots of technical equipment to make the sport safer.

ROPES AND CORDAGE

The most integral piece of equipment in the sport of climbing, whether it be cranking on crimpers up some heinously overhanging sport crag, chipping your way up a frozen water fall, or fighting your way up a Himalayan giant, is the rope. Without it, every other piece of gear becomes superfluous and, basically, useless.

The rope is a lifeline. It joins climbers together and links all the protection gear placed in the rock to form a chain that ultimately allows upward progress in a controlled and relatively safe manner.

A few decades ago a rope was a rope, but today they are manufactured to hi tech specifications for different applications.

Ropes have a core that is the main load-bearing part. Around this goes the mantle, the main purpose of which is to protect the core. Climbing ropes undergo stringent testing and have breaking strains far in excess of forces they are likely to encounter.

Climbing ropes that are used for leading are known as dynamic ropes. This means that the rope will stretch when loaded, thus absorbing the impact of a falling climber and reducing the shock load on the protection equipment and the belay stance.

Static ropes look similar to dynamic ropes, but hardly stretch at all. These ropes are more suited for hauling, abseiling (rappelling), caving and sometimes top-roping. To lead on a static rope is extremely dangerous because, without stretch, the lack of shock absorption results in much higher transmission of loads to the runners, belays and the climber's body making even a short leader fall more serious.

All climbing ropes come in different lengths, the standard being about 50–70m (165–230ft) and are divided into three main categories: Single (full strength), double (half strength) and twin ropes.

Single ropes. The diameter of a single rope can vary from 9.1mm to 11mm and they can be used on their own: official testing has concluded that a single rope is strong enough to hold leader falls.

Double ropes. The diameter of these ropes can vary from 8.5mm to 9mm. Two ropes should always be used at the same time (hence the name). However, it is acceptable to clip alternate ropes through protection gear: in the event of a fall, only one of the ropes will bear the brunt, while the other backs it up.

Dynamic rope suitable for leading.

Static rope suitable for abseiling and caving.

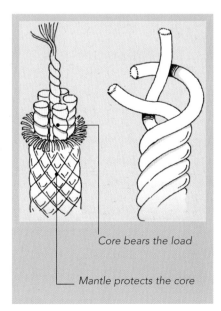

Core bears the load

Mantle protects the core

Twin ropes. These are the thinnest of all, with diameters of between 7.5mm and 8.2mm. They are designed for ice climbing and two ropes must always be used strictly as one rope: they should never be separated and must be clipped together through all pieces of gear. They do, however, allow for longer abseils.

There are many other ropes and cord of a lesser diameter for different uses. Thinner cord, (3–5mm) is often used to secure an anchor at abseil points. This is left behind once the rope is pulled. Thicker cord can be fashioned into slings of various lengths, to be used at anchor points or as running belays.

WEBBING

Most slings used today are made of different widths of webbing. Generally they come in widths of 10mm (⅜ in) to 25mm (1 in) and lengths of 600mm (24 in) to 1200mm (47 in). They are sewn and bartacked in the factory and have breaking strains in excess of 2 tons. Webbing is also available off a reel, so any length can be obtained if you wish to fashion a non-standard length of sling. Strong webbing and accessory cord is also made of hi tech fabric Spectra/Dyneema.

WIRED NUTS

Nuts (or chocks) are wedged or jammed into a crack, usually above a constriction. Ordinary engineering nuts were used originally, but today they come in asymmetric shapes that increase the placement possibilities. Nuts may be on wire or rope slings. Medium to small nuts are on wire cable, which has the advantage of being stronger and, since the wire is fairly stiff, can be placed deep in the back of cracks. Many are colour-coded for easy recognition. They come in a range of sizes and shapes, from micro nuts which are used in tiny, almost hairline, cracks to chunky wedges that can be jammed into wider cracks. Modern designs can cater for different-shaped cracks and pockets. (See placement and removal of gear, p88 .)

HELMETS

Although helmets can and do protect a climber's head in a fall, they mainly serve as a shield against falling stones and rocks. At sport crags there is less chance of loose rock falling from above, because climbers do not top out and walk around above the crag, but helmets are essential on traditional crags and bigger mountains. Most helmets are made of fibreglass or plastic. When buying, consider weight, durability and good fit. If a helmet takes a major blow it should be replaced. Plastic helmets become brittle with age and should be replaced in accordance with manufacturer's recommendations.

Left: Webbing has a breaking strain in excess of 2 tons.

Above: Wired nuts come in a range of sizes. They are tapered and curved to fit cracks and pockets of different shapes and sizes.

CAMMING DEVICES

These little guys revolutionized crack climbing in the 1970s and 80s. They were designed for parallel-sided cracks with few natural constrictions where wedges could be placed. They became popular very quickly, and you will be hard pushed to find a climber without a set on his rack. Cams come in all sizes from tiny ones that can be fiddled into 5mm (⅕ inch) seams, to huge unwieldy units that can fit into 300mm (12 in) wide cracks. They all have three or four cams which are depressed by means of a trigger. It is then inserted into a crack and the trigger is released to lock the cams up against the side of the crack. Ideally, the cams should be locked within the middle 50 per cent of their range of movement for greatest strength.

It takes practice to become proficient in placing cams. Overcamming a unit or pushing it too far into a crack can make it impossible to remove.

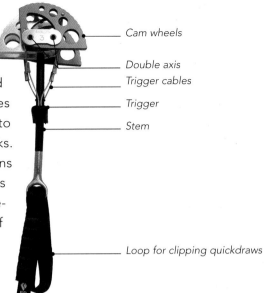

Cam wheels

Double axis

Trigger cables

Trigger

Stem

Loop for clipping quickdraws

KARABINERS

Karabiners are made of an aluminium alloy with a breaking strain in excess of 2000kg (4400 lb). There are two main types of karabiner: the locking, or screwgate type; and non-locking, or clipgate type. The main job of any karabiner is to connect two points, whether it is a sling being connected to a belay anchor, the anchor to a climber's harness, or the rope connected to a piece of protection by means of a quickdraw.

Locking karabiners. Mainly used where it is important that the karabiner should not open under any circumstances, for instance at stances for belaying, top-rope anchors and abseil points.

Snapgate karabiners. Used everywhere else in the climbing chain: connecting all pieces of protection to the rope and for attaching gear to the harness.

Minor axis

Backbar

Gate

Major axis

Bent gate karabiner

Short sling

Straight gate karabiner

QUICKDRAWS

These are very short slings with a clipgate karabiner on each end. They are used extensively in sport climbing for clipping bolts, where one karabiner is attached to the bolt and the rope is passed through the other karabiner. Quickdraws are also used in traditional climbing for the same purpose.

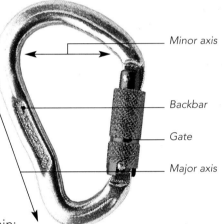

Above: A prusik loop attached to the rope with a prusik knot.

Above: Wired nuts can be difficult to remove, but a nut remover helps.

Above: A Cordelette is used to equalize the forces on anchor points.

PRUSIK LOOPS

Two lengths of 5mm cord knotted to form two separate slings: one about a metre (3ft) in length and the other half that. These thin slings can be attached to the main climbing rope using a prusik knot (see p80), which allows the slings to be slid upward, but lock under the force of a downward pull, making it possible to ascend a rope in an emergency.

NUT REMOVER

This tool is invaluable when removing a well-jammed wired nut, or a camming device. On one side it has a flat metal edge which can be used to dislodge a jammed nut, and on the other side some have two curved claws, which can be used to reach the trigger of a camming unit that has crept deep inside a crack.

CORDELETTES

These are made up with rope a few metres long and about 7mm to 9mm in diameter. It is knotted to form a large sling. This can be used at belay or top-rope anchors to equalize the load on all the anchor points with a single tie-in point. A large sewn sling can also be used for this purpose.

Big wall climbing

Routes up big, remote walls are hard work, often demanding large amounts of artificial climbing and spending days, even weeks, in the vertical playground.

Apart from all the standard gear used for climbing any traditional route, you also need specially designed equipment for a big wall.

When Warren Harding made the first ascent of the Nose on El Capitan in Yosemite Valley nearly 50 years ago, he had to make special pitons to enable him to climb a certain section. He fashioned these from the legs of an old cast iron stove – and this section subsequently became known as the Stove Leg Cracks.

Today a whole array of gear is manufactured for aid/big wall climbing. Besides the actual technical gear needed to climb the wall, other specialized equipment, such as haul bags, 'portaledges', hanging cook sets and the like are also necessary in order to spend days or weeks on the wall.

Above: A group of climbers on Zodiac – a big wall route on El Capitan in the Yosemites.

PITONS (OR PEGS)

Climbers started using pitons many years ago. Home-made metal spikes of varying sizes were driven into cracks for protection and also for aid. Today there are many different sizes and shapes of pitons from huge, hollow, angled metal (known as angles and bongs), which can be used in very wide cracks, to birdbeaks, that will bite only a few millimetres into a blind crack. Rurps (Realized Ultimate Reality Pitons) are tiny, thin blades that were developed in 1959 on Kat Pinnacle in Yosemite by legendary climber Yvon Chouinard to handle the climb's crux, a hairline crack.

PEG HAMMER

Apart from driving pitons into cracks, it is also used to bang mashies and copperheads (see p44) into depressions. Most piton hammers have a spike on the reverse end, which can be used for clearing out jammed-up cracks.

Right: Piton hammers have a flat side for hitting in the pitons, and a sharper pick for copperheads or for cleaning cracks. The hammer is attached to the harness with a sling that allows the climber full above-head extension.

Left: A selection of pitons on a bandolier (top to bottom): knifebleaks, angles, leepers, and lost arrows.

COPPERHEADS AND MASHIES

These are cylindrical copper or aluminium swages welded onto steel cable, and are used to facilitate the crossing of blank sections of rock that offer no crack lines, but do have depressions and incipient grooves. The head of the mashie is placed in a suitable depression or groove and then hammered, so that the crystals of the rock bite into the metal to give, one hopes, sufficient purchase to take a climber's bodyweight. They can not, however, hold a fall, so climbing a section of rock using a series of mashies without other reliable gear can be extremely taxing on the mind.

BAT HOOKS

These hooks are very useful for crossing blank sections of rock that have tiny horizontal edges or flakes. They can also be placed in shallow drilled holes or small pockets. A bat hook is designed in such a way that, when loaded, it tends to be pulled inward toward the rock, making the blade bite deeper. It is also used to aid the lead climber while drilling bolt holes on a blank section of rock.

Above: A bat hook can bite into a tiny edge. An etrier is then attached to it.

ETRIERS OR AIDERS

Aiders are miniature three- or four-step ladders commonly made of webbing. The top of the aider is clipped into a piece of gear, after which the climber stands in the rungs, often working his or her way up until he/she is standing in the top rung (known as 'top-runging'). The climber then places another piece of gear and repeats the process.

Below: Etriers (or aiders) are used in aid climbing to gain height.

BOLT KIT

This can be a manual kit where the drill bit is placed in a special tube and hammered manually into the rock. However, that is time consuming and tedious work with a single bolt hole taking up to an hour to drill. Once the hole is deep enough, an expansion bolt is inserted and tightened. Manual kits are generally only used when weight is an important issue on the wall. It is much easier to use a battery powered cordless drill. It allows you to place bolts in minutes, but an average drill can weigh up to 5kg (11 lb). So you have to make a decision about weight versus convenience! (Always be aware of ethical considerations about bolt use, especially in Great Britain and now in the Alps.)

Above: A typical bolt kit with cordless (battery-operated) drill and drill bits, hammer, blow tube, spanner with connecting cord, hanger and lower-off anchors.

ASCENDERS

These are mechanical clamps that are used extensively on big walls and on aid pitches. It is clamped onto the sheath of the rope and is designed so that you can slide it upward, but it will lock with any downward force. They have handles for gripping with your hands and attachment points for slings that are used for your feet and attaching to your waist. Using two ascenders a climber can 'jug' up a 50m (164ft) rope in mere minutes.

FIFI HOOK

This is a blunt open hook that is fastened to the front of the harness on the end of a short sling and allows the climber to rest in the middle of a pitch by slipping the hook through any piece of fixed gear.

Left: *A fifi hook, which is used to clip into aid gear.*

HAUL BAGS

A team of climbers attempting a route up a big wall needs to take loads of kit with them. Haul bags, commonly known as pigs, or pork sacks, are large cylindrical bags made of thick vinyl material to withstand the constant abrasion against the rock. All the gear, food, water and other supplies needed for a stint on the wall are stuffed into one or more of these bags and hauled up the route behind the climbers. This in itself can be an arduous task and special techniques and equipment are used for this.

Above: *Ascenders are mechanical clamps that lock onto the sheath of a rope, and can be pushed upwards. They are used for rapid ascent.*

Right: *Haul bags are obligatory on any big wall climb. This is the bag where you stash all your food, water, clothing, sleeping, cooking gear and anything else deemed necessary. It is hauled up the face behind the climbers after each pitch. Haulbags are made of hardwearing material to be able to withstand the abrasion caused by continuous hauling.*

PULLEYS AND WALL HAULERS

These are used to haul bags up a big wall. Wall haulers are better in that they have a brake action that allows the person doing the hauling to release the rope. The brake will lock the system and hauling can be continued at will.

Right: *A pulley, which is used to facilitate hauling bags up big walls.*

COOKING GEAR

Big wall cook sets are designed to be hung from fixed gear because there is seldom anywhere to place a stove or pot. The pots are designed to fit into each other and also to fit into the stove housing.

CLOTHING

Climbing big walls is particularly hard on your hands and knees so, besides your normal kit, you need gloves (fingerless leather ones are most common) and padding to protect your knees from the continuous grating against the rock during a long climb. Also important are comfortable shoes. These days a good pair of 'approach' shoes are more than adequate; they are designed for a comfortable fit, have a sticky sole and some even have high ankle support.

TOILET EQUIPMENT

Bowel movements on a big wall are not a simple matter. Gone are the days of letting loose from an exposed perch and sending your wastes to an airy grave. Today most big wall climbers use a poop tube. This is a cylindrical PVC tube about 50cm (20 in) long. It is sealed at one end with an airtight lid that can be opened to allow bags of faeces to be pushed in and compressed down. Once off the route the content is dispatched down a toilet – NOT IN A GARBAGE CAN.

PORTALEDGES AND SLEEPING GEAR

Portaledges are tents with a ridged floor designed to be used on a vertical wall. Many big walls have vast sweeps of rock bereft of any ledges, let alone one big enough to sleep on. Portaledges can be rigged up anywhere on a wall from fixed gear placed by the climber. They come in single and double sizes.

The rest of the sleeping gear, such as sleeping bags, are much the same as you would use anywhere else in the outdoors given the same weather conditions.

Right: A climber relaxing on a portaledge set up against a steep wall that has no ledges to sleep on.

Above: *Climbers on a big wall need a great deal of paraphernalia, including, for environmental reasons, the obligatory poop tube on the right.*

Above: *A hanging stove with compatible pot systems are used on big walls where there is seldom a ledge to rest a butt cheek, let alone a stove.*

Ice and Snow

Because of their ever-changing nature, climbing on ice and snow can be complex and requires specialized equipment.

Crampons: It would be foolish and dangerous to venture onto any relatively hard snow or ice surface in the mountains without a pair of crampons strapped firmly to your boots.

A crampon is a metal framework, with eight or ten sharp spikes protruding downward and two protruding from the front (for kicking into steep surfaces). They can be either strapped on or clipped to the soles of mountaineering boots. There are many different styles depending on the type of climbing being done.

Ice Axe: Ice axes come in many shapes and sizes, depending on the sort of climbing you intend to do.

Simple glacier crossings do not need technical axes. A standard long-shafted axe will be more than adequate. Venturing onto steeper ground or frozen waterfalls calls for futuristic designs with shorter shafts and interchangeable picks and adzes to allow for versatility. The strongest, and best, shafts are made of aluminium alloy or carbon fibre. The handle should be coated with rubber for insulation and grip.

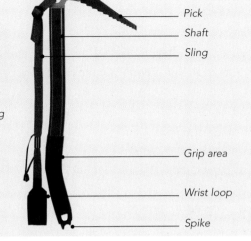

Right: A standard long-shafted ice axe is adequate for glacier crossings. However, ice climbing on frozen waterfalls require specially designed axes.

Adze/hammer
Pick
Shaft
Sling
Grip area
Wrist loop
Spike

ICE PROTECTION

Protection placed in ice and snow can only be as good as the medium itself.

Ice Screws: A well-placed ice screw in solid ice can provide excellent protection with a holding force of up to 2000kg (4410 lb). However, anything placed in rotten ice is almost useless.

Deadmen: These are metal plates of about 20–25cm^2 (3–4 sq in) that can be pounded into the ice to provide an anchor. If placed correctly, any force exerted onto the deadman through the cable to which it is attached, will draw the device deeper into the ice.

Ice Stake: These are metal stakes about 45–90cm (18–35 in) long, with V- or T-shaped shafts. They are driven into the ice or snow to serve as anchors.

Right: Ice screws come in different sizes and have tremendous holding force in good ice. In bad ice it is worthless.

Above: A deadman is a spade-shaped alloy plate, with a long wire attached to its centre. If well placed, any force exerted on the wire will drive the spade in deeper.

Left: Modern step-in semi-rigid 12-point crampons. They are also available as fully rigid, or 10-point models.

Right: Ice stakes serve as anchors.

PROTECTIVE CLOTHING

The sport of climbing is practised in all conditions: from
climbing a 50m (164ft) frozen
waterfall on a sunny day only 20
minutes' walk from your car to
crossing the second ice field on
the north face of the Eiger with
storm clouds billowing around
your head, or edging your way
up a teetering pile of mixed
ground 8000m (26,000ft) up. And
each scenario will require a different combination of protective
clothing. However, the basic
principle will always be to keep
dry; keep the wind out; and
dress in layers.

Above: *A down jacket should zip up to cover the neck area, have overlapping seams to keep out the wind, a hood with an adjustable opening for the face and sealed-off cuffs.*

Above: *Boots should be waterproof, sturdy and offer ankle support. When checking for fit, ensure that you can stuff a finger behind your heel while wearing a thin and thick pair of socks. Also check for crampon compatibility if you intend to do the kind of climbing that requires them.*

COLD WEATHER CLOTHING CHECKLIST

In cold conditions it is important to wear clothing in layers. Air is a good insu-
lator and layered clothing allows air pockets to form where warm air can be
trapped. For the same reason it is important to have wind-proof clothing that
will prevent the warm air from being blown away. Here is a basic list of clothing that can be used at varying levels of extreme weather. It is by no means
comprehensive and many climbers have their own permutations.

• Base layer – polypropylene long john pants and long sleeve top
• First layer – 100 weight fleece top
• Wind-stop fleece trousers and heavier wind-stop fleece top (300 weight)
• Down jacket with hood (and down trousers in extreme conditions)
• Waterproof, breathable shell (top and bottom)
• Wind-stop fleece gloves
• Waterproof, breathable over-gloves
• Wind-stop balaclava
• Warm, waterproof boots
• A good pair of sunglasses or snow goggles (vital).

BIVVY EQUIPMENT

The dilemma often pondered when planning a big route is whether to go light and fast or prepared for the worst, but slow. If you weigh yourself down with bivvy (bivouac) gear you will almost certainly end up having to use it. On the other hand, if you go light and fast (*sans* bivvy gear) and get it wrong, you may have to spend a long, cold night with one frozen butt cheek stuck to a sloping, ice-encrusted ledge. Taking bivvy gear or not is your choice, but if you do decide to pack in the kit make sure it's the right stuff for the route you are planning to climb. Bivvy gear needed for an Alpine push on an 8000m (26,000ft) peak can be very different to gear needed for a route on one of the north faces in the European Alps, or a big wall on Baffin Island.

Above: *In the mountains the weather often forces you to cook inside a tent. Ensure reasonable air circulation and that your stove and pots are stable.*

BIVVY CHECKLIST

Tent – for Himalayan style bivvys
Sleeping bags
Bivvy sacs (breathable, waterproof)
Groundsheet
Sleeping pad (or one to sit on)
Hand and foot warmers
Headlamps
Cooking gear

Right: *A bivvy sac offers the protection of a tent, but is extremely lightweight.*

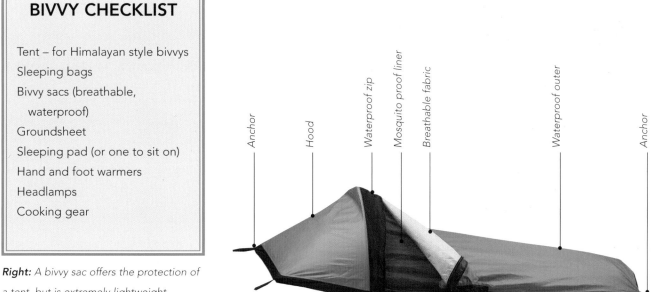

Anchor · Hood · Waterproof zip · Mosquito proof liner · Breathable fabric · Waterproof outer · Anchor

Equipment care and maintenance

Great care is taken in the manufacture of climbing equipment, the majority of which undergoes stringent testing to ensure climber safety. It is, however, important for safety reasons, as well as the cost of replacement, that climbers look after and maintain their gear. Some items, like ropes, slings and shoes have to be replaced at regular intervals, because they wear out faster than hardware like karabiners, camming units and wired nuts. However, looking after your gear can add years of use to rope and karabiner alike.

ROPES, SLINGS AND CORDAGE

Rope is your lifeline and should be treated as such.

- Always store out of harm's way.
- Never leave it lying around near corrosive materials like battery acid or oils that could be found in the boot of a car. This will eat away the nylon, rendering the rope useless.
- Avoid leaving rope in direct sunlight, since ultraviolet radiation weakens the nylon.
- Never stand on a rope. There could be sharp stones underneath, or grit could be forced between the fibres and damage the rope.
- When climbing at a crag, a rope tarpaulin will keep the rope off the ground and out of the dirt.
- Avoid running your rope over sharp edges or rough surfaces.
- When top-roping or abseiling (rappelling) make sure your rope clears the edge of the crag.

- Inspect your rope regularly for abrasions. If the core is visible through the mantle, then either cut out the damaged section, or discard the rope.
- Keep track of how many falls your rope has taken. A rope should be discarded if it has held a major fall.
- Ropes can be washed in warm water with a mild soap. Not all ropes get washed in their lifetime, but if ropes are pulled through muddy ground, then it is advisable to wash them. The same applies to ropes that have been lying on the ground in sand and grit over extended periods (months) without the protection of a rope bag. Washing them removes grit and dirt particles from the inside of the strands, where they can damage the rope.
- A lead rope should not be used for more than five years. If subjected to heavy usage, it should be replaced sooner.

KARABINERS

Karabiners can last 10 years or longer if they are looked after.

- Do not drop or throw karabiners around. This can cause hairline fractures impossible to see, but that greatly reduce the strength of a karabiner.
- Climbing near the sea can cause your karabiners to become stiff and the gates may seize up. In this case a light lubrication usually does the trick. Use WD40, or cooking oil as this is non toxic and kind to climbing gear. Graphite lubricant is best.

Check rope for abrasions. It should never be so worn that the core becomes visible.

A rope bag and unfolding tarpaulin will protect the rope from sand and grit.

A rope being pulled over a sharp edge will damage the mantle.

A karabiner is weakened by three-way loading.

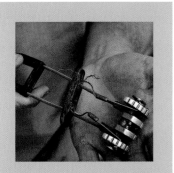

A camming unit showing frayed and broken cable strands.

Sand and grit can damage the soles of your climbing shoes. Take them off when not climbing.

Avoid a three-way pull on karabiners, or loading them over an edge, because this can damage them and increase the risk of the gate opening accidentally.

WIRED NUTS

These are quite hardy pieces of gear, but they can be damaged while being removed from a tricky placement: yanking the cables can cause the wire threads to kink near the nut itself, which can weaken the unit as a whole and also cause individual strands to break.

CAMMING UNITS

Cams are probably the most expensive bits of hardware you will buy. They are complex pieces of gear with many working parts that rely on smooth movement. Stiff and sticky cams are dangerous and irritating to operate. To remedy stiff cams, lubricate them with cooking oil or spray WD40 between the working parts. Try to keep them off the ground where they can pick up grit and sand. Inspect the cables that connect the pull lever to the cam wheels regularly for broken strands. Although this does not affect the strength of the unit, it can affect its operation.

ROCK SHOES

If you climb a lot you will probably spend more on shoes than any other equipment. It is not unusual to go through two pairs per year if you climb more than two or three days a week. Looking after your shoes will make them last longer and give better performance.

When storing your shoes, stuff paper down into the toe box to help keep the shape of the shoe, and avoid cramming them into your pack beneath other gear that will crush and distort them.

Only wear your shoes when absolutely necessary: only when climbing, not before and not after. Never walk around at the base of the crag in your climbing shoes, since grit and sand corrode the rubber and reduce the friction properties. Always check that your soles are totally free of dirt before you set foot on the rock. Also make sure that your feet are clean when wearing your shoes. Dirty feet will make the insides of your shoes dirty and slimy.

When your soles or rand wear out, they can be repaired by specialist climbing shoe resolers.

HELMETS

Keep your helmet clean, avoid dropping it, and replace it after a major impact. Replace plastic helmets at least every five years.

GENERAL CARE

All climbing gear should be stored in a cool, dry place and away from harmful chemicals like household detergents and motorcar lubricants. Inspect your gear at regular intervals to make sure that everything is in good condition. Harnesses should be inspected for loose stitching and abrasions.

Loads and resistances

It is said that climbing ropes never break, they only cut (due to poor practices). Climbing ropes are made much stronger than necessary, and could be made even stronger, but the strength of a climbing rope is not the only important factor. Its ability to absorb the impact force of a falling climber is equally important. Most single climbing ropes have a breaking strain in excess of 2000kg (4410 lb) – much more than the forces generated by a fall.

The ideal climbing rope should be light, flexible, strong, able to absorb multiple impact forces, and have good handling qualities. Fortunately today, due to modern technology, many ropes have all these qualities.

The rope's ability to absorb the energy of a fall depends on how much it stretches, and this in turn determines part of the impact force of a fall. Other criteria that determine the forces generated in a fall are how much rope is involved in the fall and, of course, the height (length) of the fall itself.

To help us understand the forces involved in a fall and how to avoid the dangers of high impact forces, the concept of fall factors was devised. The fall factor is the length of a fall divided by the length of the rope active during the fall. This means that fall factors can only range between 0 and 2. A fall factor of 2 constitutes a fall with the most impact force, and is considered very serious.

To avoid high fall factors, you need to place enough protection to keep the fall factor at an acceptable level (less than 1). This is easier said than done: on many difficult routes it is not possible to place protection at frequent intervals; and since not all gear is bombproof, some of it is ripped from the rock during a fall, adding to the length of the fall and increasing the fall factor.

The more experienced the leader, the better the chance of keeping the fall factors down to acceptable levels.

Cam

Rule 1: Place gear near the stance. The lead climber has placed a cam soon after leaving the stance.

Rule 2: Place gear regularly. The length of your fall is determined by the proximity of your last piece of protection.

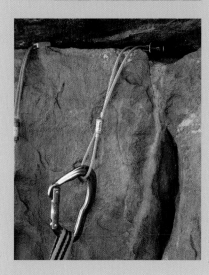

Rule 3: Back up crucial gear. Before tackling a blank section or a series of hard moves place more than one piece of gear.

THREE RULES THAT HELP AVOID HIGH FALL FACTORS.

Rule 1: Place gear before you leave the stance, or as soon as possible afterward. This way you have immediately removed the chance of a factor 2 fall.

Rule 2: Never pass up the opportunity to place good gear. With every piece of gear placed the fall factor is reduced.

Rule 3: Always back up crucial or suspect pieces of gear, or when approaching the crux section. If one piece rips out, the other should hold the fall, thereby keeping the fall factor from increasing.

WHAT HAPPENS DURING A FALL

While fall factors do help us understand what happens during a fall, the concept does not give us the complete picture as these examples illustrate:

Example 1: You are 50m (165ft) above the stance with your last piece of gear a frightening 10m (33ft) below your feet. A fall at this point would mean a drop of 20m (66ft), excluding rope stretch. This gives a relatively low fall factor of 0.4.

Example 2: You are only 15m (50ft) above the stance with your last piece of gear a nervous 5m (16ft) below you. A fall at this moment would mean a fall of 10m (33ft), giving a fall factor of almost 0.7.

However, neither example takes into account the speed at which the falling climber will be travelling at point of impact, nor that

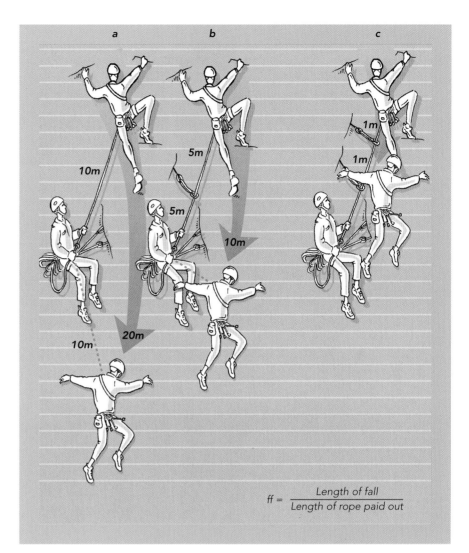

$$ff = \frac{Length\ of\ fall}{Length\ of\ rope\ paid\ out}$$

Above: Three examples illustrating how fall factors are calculated. The equation is: the length of the fall divided by the length of rope between the belayer and the climber.

a) The climber is 10m above the belayer with no protection. A fall here means the climber will fall 10+10m = 20m. And $\frac{20}{10}$ gives a fall factor of 2.

b) The climber is 10m above the belayer with protection out at 5m. A fall here means the climber will fall 5+5m = 10m. And $\frac{10}{10}$ gives a fall factor of 1.

c) The climber is 10m above the belayer with two pieces of protection, the highest one being only 1m below the climber. A fall here means the climber will fall 1+1m = 2m. And $\frac{2}{10}$ gives a fall factor of 0.2.

there is a higher chance of the climber in the first example hitting protrusions during the fall, due to the length of the fall. The climber in the second example has a fall factor almost double that of the climber in the first, but the climber in the first example will fall double the distance and have a greater terminal velocity.

Above: A sport climber's rack is simple and lightweight, comprising 10-12 quickdraws. How you arrange them on your harness is a matter of personal preference. Most climbers prefer to have the shorter quickdraws towards the front, and the longer ones further back. Some prefer the karabiner gate facing outward, while others prefer it to face inward.

Equipment in the bag

A day at a sport crag involves a different bag of tricks to a day on a serious multi-pitch trad route high in the mountains, far from the fleshpots of civilization.

SPORT CRAG

To me a day at the local sport crag means a short walk from the car, a high fun factor, with the minimum of risk and a reasonably low fear count. So what goes in the rucksack apart from all the standard sport climbing paraphernalia? Tea of course. In goes the old flask, or cooker with all the necessary ingredients. Next would be some food, like pastries or sandwiches. This already makes for a fun day in the hills, even if you weren't climbing. Next is a warm fleece, a waterproof top and a beanie to keep your brain from freezing. That way, even if it does rain and you have to can the climbing, you can go for a walk and still have a great day on the hill. And don't forget to pop a few quid in your pocket for a pint at the local later that evening.

LONG MULTIPITCH TRADITIONAL OR ALPINE ROUTE

This requires a totally different mind-set. Although fun is always supposed to be part of the equation, it is easy to lose your sense of humour when hypothermia is threatening to set in, or night is falling and you are still three pitches from the top of the route and your partner is expecting you home for dinner.

Packing your sack for a day (or two) in the mountains, with the intention of doing a long trad route, requires more thought and is usually done in conjunction with your climbing partner. Weight and sack space become an issue.

Food must be carefully thought out. High-energy snacks are good, with some extras just in case the day unexpectedly becomes night. Warm protective clothing is essential. Consider packing a small stove and a few tea bags. A cup of hot tea can warm you up and restore your sanity during a long, cold night stuck on some ledge in the middle of a wall.

A cellphone (mobile) is a must if there is coverage. In an emergency, a telephone call can shave hours off the time needed to alert a rescue team, which can, sometimes, mean the difference between life and death. And if you are unexpectedly benighted, a call home can make all the difference to loved ones awaiting your return. Another important item, which is often left out, is a headlamp – not a hand-held torch – a headlamp, that leaves your hands free. This could mean the difference between spending the night on the hill, or being able to return to your car after nightfall and going home to a hot bath, a single malt whisky and a scrumptious meal. Just think about it.

Above: *Climbers sorting through their rack and equipment in preparation for a serious route of alpine proportions.*

ESSENTIAL SKILLS AND TECHNIQUES

So many times have I heard: 'Gee, you must be really strong to pull yourself up a vertical wall.' And therein lies the error. If all you are doing is pulling yourself, then you are going to get tired very quickly and within a short distance your arms will give in and you will fall. Climbing is not all about strength and burly moves up a steep wall. On the contrary. Climbing is an art, a vertical chess game that has to be worked out by means of good balance, technique and applied strategy. As a beginner, one should never favour strength training over practising good technique. Good footwork will keep the weight off your arms and over your feet. Your legs are ten times stronger than your arms, so let them do the work.

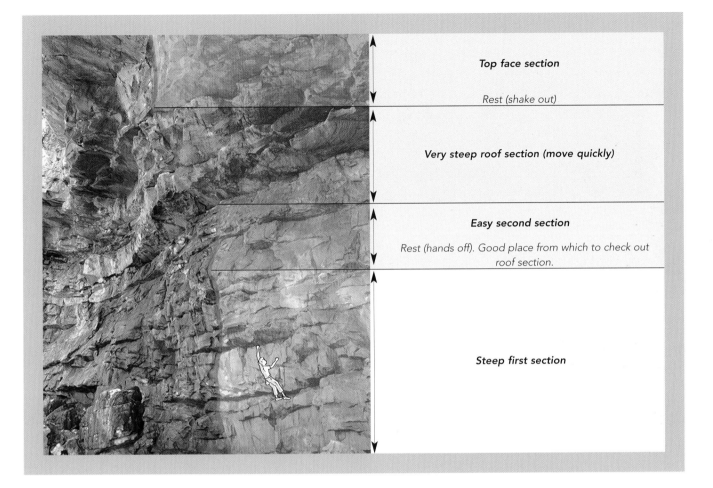

Top face section

Rest (shake out)

Very steep roof section (move quickly)

Easy second section

Rest (hands off). Good place from which to check out roof section.

Steep first section

Being strong helps, of course, but being able to recognize and pull off a series of moves by applying good technique will get you much further.

Ability and strength are all very well, but there is one more factor that overrules everything and which, if you don't have it under control, you may as well pack your bags and go fishing: the mind. It is the most powerful weapon in your climbing arsenal. Good mind control will improve technique, strength and endurance. (See also chapter 12, Preparation and Training).

Moving on rock

A rock climb is basically a series of moves executed in a specific sequence. Getting the sequence right is the tricky part. The route should first be checked out in its entirety, then broken down into climbable chunks, separated by good resting places. Identifying good rest spots can make the difference between success and failure. Once you have decided where your rests are going to be, take each section between the rests and break them down into individual moves. Check out what kind of hand holds and foot holds

are on offer, and how you can use them. This will determine your sequences. Try and visualize yourself using the holds and how you would position your body while doing so; then how you would link one set of holds to another, always keeping in mind footwork and body position. All this is called 'reading the rock', the importance of which cannot be stressed enough.

Getting it wrong on your first attempt is quite normal. If this is the case, then work out the moves hanging from the rope, until you have it sussed. Sometimes it can take many attempts and different sequences to figure out the right way. This is all part of the game.

Listen to more experienced climbers. While you are up there, gripped out of your mind, feet flailing and in the process of falling off, an experienced climber may be trying to help you by offering advice: where to put your right foot, or how to overcome a troublesome bulge by using a hidden undercling hold. Often a little advice from the right source can make an impossible sequence seem trivial.

Try never to get more pumped (loss of strength associated with overworked muscles) than necessary, which is easier said than done, of course, but with strong mental control this can be achieved.

Always start the route in a clear, relaxed frame of mind and try to keep it that way throughout the pitch. A nervous climber tends to climb jerkily, often neglecting precise footwork, thereby putting unnecessary strain on the arms. A touch of nerves will also make you grip the rock harder than you need to, expending valuable energy, making you pump out more quickly.

Placing gear on a steep climb can sap your strength rapidly. Try to arrange your gear in the order you will need it on the pitch, or at least for the steep section of a pitch, before you get there. This way little time is wasted on selecting the right piece. Simply slot it in and move quickly through the strenuous section.

Not getting enough reach to execute the move

Hugging the rock too closely

Standing flat-footed

Good body positioning gives climber enough reach to execute move

Leaning back gives the climber a good view of holds above.

Foot up – ensures good balance

Standing on tip-toes for better reach

Top: Bad style – keeping the feet flat, hugging the rock and not getting enough reach.
Above: Good style – getting the feet up, leaning away from the rock for a clear view.

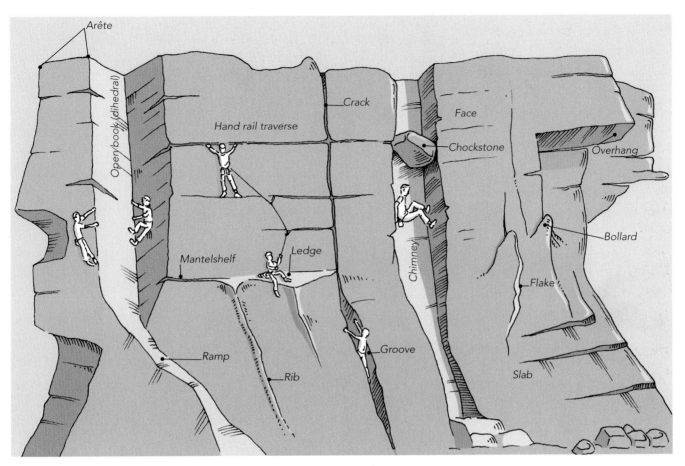

Above: Climbers need to know the best techniques to climb the different features of a rock face .

Slab climbing

Slabs are low-angled faces of around 60° to 80°. A slab liberally sprinkled with good holds is relatively easy to climb: being less than vertical, little arm strength is needed but, without good holds, it is less easy. Good balance is critical on steep, smooth slabs, as are confidence in your footwork and trust in the friction properties of the soles of your climbing shoes. Always try to stand as upright as possible. Leaning into the slab will give you a false sense of security while making it harder for your shoes to grip on the surface. Try to take small steps, since high-stepping can put you off balance and also make it difficult to execute the move. If you have to take a big step up, a good option would be to try and 'rock over' (see p65) onto the hold. This means shifting the weight of your body over the foot that is doing the high step. Always keep a look-out for bumps, pockets and rugosities on slabs, since this can make difficult moves a lot easier. Although many climbers shrug off slabs as a waste of time, it is here that you develop and maintain the foot control needed for climbs of all angles.

Face climbing

Face climbing is probably one of the most enjoyable forms of climbing, but can also be the hardest to figure out. Climbing a face is never as obvious as simply following a crack, for instance. It can have you weaving from side to side trying to link moves and piece together sequences that will enable you to make upward progress. Face climbing can throw many different kinds of holds at you, which means pulling all sorts of varying techniques out of the bag to solve the puzzle.

OVERHANGS AND ROOFS

Overhangs can be intimidating. This is mainly because you know that you have a limited time to figure out the moves before your arms start screaming. Again, always try to figure out as much as you can from the ground. Try to get a good rest to let your arms recover, just before the start of the bulge or horizontal roof. Once you have decided on a plan of action, try and move as quickly as possible through the bulge, thereby stacking the odds in your favour. Of course, this is often easier said than done. Here are some tips that can help:

• Find a crack at the start of a roof, or an edge midway along the underside of the roof, which will allow you to use an undercling hold. This then enables you to lean out further and perhaps reach over the lip of the roof. Always try to get your feet high up under the roof. This allows you more reach with your hands, which then gives you more choice of hand holds above the roof.

• The heel-hook is another technique that is often used when climbing through roofs. Once you have latched suitable holds on the lip of the roof, it can help a great deal to swing one leg over the lip and try to get purchase with the heel above, or alongside your hands, using an edge or a scoop of sorts. This takes a lot of weight off your arms and allows you to reach higher with your hands.

1. *The climber establishes herself under the roof and reaches out to the lip.*

2. *Feet are moved up to help reach better hand holds above the roof.*

3. *Hands are worked up to allow a foot to be brought up over the lip.*

4. *A foot is brought up to a hold over the lip of the roof.*

5. *The climber rocks over onto the foot and brings up the other foot.*

6. *The climber stands comfortably on the wall above the roof.*

LAYBACKS

Most moves where hands and feet use opposing forces (for instance, pulling with the arms while pushing with the feet) are layaway moves. Laybacking is simply a number of layaway moves stacked on top of each other. The most common form of layback is climbing a crack in an open-book corner, where the hands grasp and pull on the edge of the crack in the one wall, while the feet push against the wall facing you. The feet need to be near the level of the hands, so that the pull can counter the push. However, the closer your feet get to your hands, the more unstable your position. Although highly effective, this is quite strenuous, especially if the wall on which the feet are placed has few or no edges, so that the feet have to be placed high in order to stay in contact with the rock. A good tip is to look for holds behind you: even a tiny edge can allow you to stem (bridge) the corner by 'straddling' it with a foot on each wall to give your arms a much-needed break.

Laybacking is often used to climb open features like a flake, (thin slab of rock partially detached from the main face). However, without a side wall against which to maintain stability you can find yourself off balance and swing out or 'barn-door'. To counter this, place one foot further out toward the direction off the swing. Body tension can also help, especially when trying to layback an arête (a narrow ridge), where the barn-door factor can be very high. You can help keep your body where you want it to be by applying tension to the muscles in your abdomen. Lack of body tension will allow your body to swing in the wrong direction.

STEMMING (BRIDGING)

When climbing corners and wide chimneys you can straddle the gap by placing a foot on each wall. This is called stemming or bridging. Although arms are also sometimes used, the technique mainly exerts tremendous strain on the legs and hips, particularly if the walls are far apart and have no suitable foot holds, so that you have to rely mainly on the friction between your shoes and the rock. By creative stemming, -

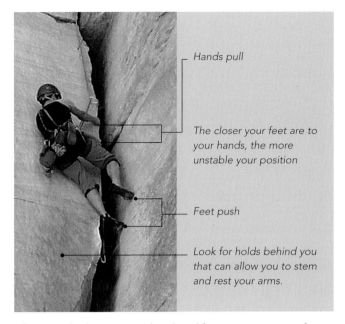

Hands pull

The closer your feet are to your hands, the more unstable your position

Feet push

Look for holds behind you that can allow you to stem and rest your arms.

Above: *Laybacking requires hands and feet to use opposing forces.*

Above: *Climber in a typical stemming position in a wide chimney.*

overhanging grooves and corners can also be climbed with little strain on the arms. Often you will also be able to find a cunning rest stop by stemming across a gap of sorts and relieve your aching forearms. A good example of this can be found on limestone crags where tufa formations hang down and away from the main wall, giving the climber good opportunities to stem one leg across the void and milk a much needed rest.

Chimneys

Although not really relished by most climbers, chimneys are often the only way through a section of rock that would be otherwise unclimbable. So, love them or hate them, learning more about chimneying techniques can make climbing them more enjoyable.

Chimneys come in many shapes and sizes, but generally there are two sizes that will accept standard chimneying techniques and two sizes that allow for upward progress, but require strenuous and awkward techniques.

1. The back-and-foot width: This is probably the easiest and most comfortable chimney to climb. The width of the fissure is such that the climber can fit in easily and be able to rest the back against the one wall and put both feet up against the other wall. Slightly narrower chimneys can also be climbed like this, but by using the knees instead of the feet.

2. Stemming width: This type of chimney is too wide for the back-and-foot method. Here you straddle the gap by placing each foot on opposite walls

(see p61). Depending on the features of the walls (foot holds, ridges or smooth) this method can be easy or very strenuous.

3. Off-width: This is the most feared and hated of all chimneys. In fact, it is the most hated of all techniques. This is a chimney that is too narrow to allow the body inside, but too wide to allow conventional crack climbing techniques like hand jams or finger locks.

To climb an off-width chimney a number of techniques can be used, all of them strenuous and unpleasant.

- **Arm bars** (used in narrow off-widths): Insert one arm in the crack and apply pressure with the palm of the hand to one side of the crack, using the top of the same arm and shoulder to push against the opposite wall. Use the other hand to grab the edge of the same side of the crack against which the palm of the other hand is pushing. This exerts forces in the right direction. Using your feet creatively, upward movement is possible.
- **Arm locks** (used in slightly wider off-widths): More or less the same as an

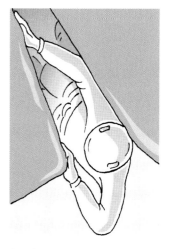
Arm bar

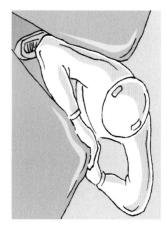
Arm lock

Shoulder lock

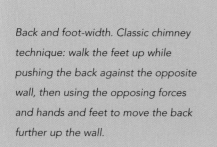
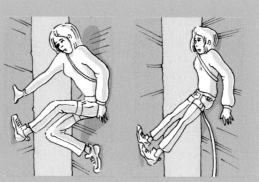
Back and foot-width. Classic chimney technique: walk the feet up while pushing the back against the opposite wall, then using the opposing forces and hands and feet to move the back further up the wall.

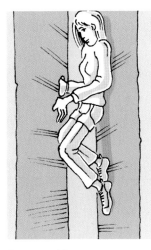

Squeeze chimney

T-Bar. Footwork in a squeeze chimney

Armwork in a squeeze chimney

arm bar, but here the arm that is inserted into the crack is bent. So the elbow points into the crack and both hands are grasping the same edge of the crack.

- **Shoulder locks:** This technique is used when the chimney is just too narrow for your body. You may fit in part of your hip and ribcage, but no more. Place a bent arm, elbow up, into the crack and place the palm against the opposite wall. After moving up, the friction of your semi-jammed body should stop you from slithering back down again. Repeat the move as many times as needed to complete the crack.

4. Squeeze chimneys: Any chimney into which you can barely fit your body, but is just a tad too wide for a heel-toe foot jam, is a squeeze chimney. They can be extremely strenuous to climb and, to make matters worse, they can also be flared. Let's look at some techniques used to climb these cracks.

- **Footwork:** If the width is right, try and stack your feet (T-bar). Opposing pressures between your feet and knees can also be used.
- **Armwork:** Off-width techniques can be used for the arms, depending on the width. A palms-out downward push can also be used to good effect. Often, one will try to edge deeper into the chimney, since the feeling of security is greater. This is never a wise move, because most squeeze chimneys get narrower the deeper you go. Stay on the outside, move slowly and never get frantic, since this will only make matters worse.

Cracks

An expedition attempting a new route on a big wall, or a climber spying a line on his local crag, will always check out the crack systems. Cracks are a natural weakness and are there to be climbed. They form the basis of all climbing. Good crack techniques will lead to many worthwhile mountain experiences. However, it is quite common to find strong sport climbers, who can crank high grades on face climbs, quiver and quake their way up a relatively easy crack line. Strength alone, without good technique, will leave you a gibbering, pumped wreck.

No one crack is the same as another and a variety of different techniques are used to climb them, depending on the crack. Cracks also mean runners, which is vital for trad climbers.

Thin cracks, which are almost seams, need good finger-locking technique (see p64) and demand difficult footwork, while wider cracks can be climbed on solid full finger locks, or hand jams (see p64).

Don't be fooled, though. The width of the crack is not the only factor; the shape is equally important. Flared cracks can leave you desperate, because finding a secure jam is nigh-on impossible, while other cracks can be knobbly inside, making jamming awkward or painful.

A good grounding in the art of jamming is essential and can make your climbing life a lot easier in many cases. There are several different kinds of handjams and fingerlocks that can be used, depending on the width of the crack.

Hand jam

Fist jam

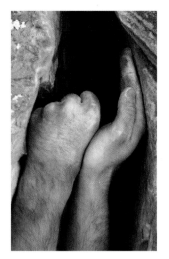

Stacked hand and fist jam for
an off-width crack

Finger lock

HAND JAMS

This is the most common form of jamming. The ideal crack size for using this technique is about 6–7cm (2½–3 in), although this will vary, depending on hand size. Insert the open hand into the crack, then make a cup, with the fingertips and heel of the hand pushing against the one side of the crack and the knuckles pushing against the other side. Tuck your thumb hard up against your index finger, or even slip it underneath, inside the palm. You will have to make slight adjustments depending on the width of the crack and irregularities inside the crack. At first this jam may feel precarious, but with practice it will become your best friend and the most secure hold you could wish for.

Fist Jam: This is used in slightly wider cracks. Once the hand is inserted into the crack a fist is made and the hand turned sideways allowing the sides of the hand to jam against the sides of the crack. The fist can face up or down, depending on the feel. The fist jam, unlike the hand jam, rarely feels totally secure and needs a lot of practice. Always look for a constriction above which to jam. This will improve its security.

Off-width hands: The crack that is just too wide for a decent hand jam, is often the most feared. A different technique is needed to climb these horror shows. For these wider cracks, try stacking two hands together, or a stacked hand and fist jam. These jams will rarely feel secure, but can still do the trick when all else fails.

FINGER LOCKS

Finger cracks vary in width from shallow seams that only accept the tips of your fingers to cracks into which you can stuff your fingers to the palm. What they have in common is that you will have to execute painful finger locks in a strenuous position. All finger locks require the climber to torque the fingers to some degree. With a few rare exceptions all cracks have irregularities; you need to look for these slight constrictions to make the finger lock more secure. If pulling straight down on a tenuous finger lock feels precarious, try shifting your body to one side. This often makes a difference. Or try placing your fingers with the index finger pointing down. This can help to make a bad lock feel snug.

Other finger locks: Some cracks are only just wide enough to accept the very tips of your fingers, or maybe only the tip of your little finger, making for very dubious locking moves. Others are a little too wide for a comfortable finger lock and here a thumb stack can

Rockover: the foot is placed on the hold and the body shifted across and up until your weight is directly above the foot.

Dyno: Poised to jump, eyes focused on upper hold. The climber lunges, losing all contact with the rock and latches onto the hold.

often do the trick. Put your thumbs into the crack – if necessary, one on top of the other – then torque them to lock in. Alternatively, jam your thumbs in alongside each other.

FOOTWORK

As mentioned before, you will go nowhere fast if you neglect your foot technique. No matter how good the jams, if your footwork is shoddy, your arms will tire, and you will pop out of the crack like the proverbial cork.

When climbing cracks, whether conventional or off-width, always look for foot holds outside, or just inside the crack. These can give your arms a break from the strenuous work that most cracks demand. Some cracks, however, like those of Canyon Lands in Utah, USA, can be splitter cracks that cleave a blank sandstone wall with nary a foot nor hand hold anywhere.

Foot jamming is the only way to climb those cracks. The foot is turned sideways, inserted into the crack and torqued downward to lock into the crack. These can be anything from thin toe jams to solid foot jams across the ball of your foot. Jamming of all kinds (foot or hand) is not easy and lots of practice is needed to perfect it; don't be disillusioned if your first jam crack feels 10 grades harder than the book says. Keep plugging away, you will slowly get the hang of it.

Whole body moves
ROCK OVERS

This is a high step, where the hand holds above are not very good. The foot is placed on the hold and your body is shifted across and up, until your weight is directly above the foot. Once in balance it is possible to stand up on that foot. Little friction jumps with the other foot can help with the upward movement.

DYNAMIC MOVE (DYNO)

On certain sports routes, these days, you will be unable to move up to the next hold with conventional techniques. The dyno is an explosive move that catapults the climber from a hold, past the blank section, to latch onto a hold above. This should be executed in a controlled and calculated manner. A dyno can be a short move, where the bottom hand is still on the bottom hold when the top hand is slapping the top hold, or it can be a full body dyno, where the hands and feet lose all contact with the rock while the body is propelled upward to latch the next hold several metres away. It is important to visualize the move and the hold that you are going for. Move with confidence. Never execute a dyno half-heartedly, or you will flail hopelessly and head for a downward plunge. (It should not be used on poorly protected trad routes.)

MANTELLING

1. Heave yourself up as if getting out of a swimming pool until you can push down.

2. Push down with your hands until you can get one foot on top of the shelf.

3. With one foot on the ledge you can push up until you can reach a handhold above.

4. Pull yourself onto the ledge.

LOCKING OFF

When a climber pulls up and has to release one hand to reach up for the next hold, it is called a lock-off. The other arm then locks off to hold the climber in a static position. It is usually very strenuous, since the arm is locked off in a bent position. This can be aggravated if the foot holds are small and the wall is steep.

MANTELLING

The technique used to gain a ledge, or even a hold, from below with scant holds above is descriptive of a person climbing onto the top of a mantel shelf. First grab the ledge with your hands, heave yourself up until your weight is balanced over your hands and you can get one foot on top of the ledge. Balance and push up until you are able to stand. The trick is not to fall backwards. A mantel is generally performed on large features, but in extreme cases you can find yourself mantelling onto tiny edges. The smaller the surface and the more it slopes, the harder you will find the mantel.

DROP-KNEE

Also known as the Egyptian, the drop-knee is a relatively modern technique where the body is twisted to the side, the knee closest to the wall is bent and

Above: The drop knee, or Egyptian, technique brings the hip closer to the wall, allowing for greater reach.

Above: With the figure 4 technique you can lever your body higher for greater reach.

GENERAL FOOT TECHNIQUES

Footwork should be precise and accurate. It is a pleasure to watch climbers with good footwork: they seem to glide effortlessly over the rock compared to someone with bad foot work, who climbs in a jerky manner.

- Look where you are placing your feet rather than scrape and feel your way blindly up the rock.
- Lean out so that the foot holds are visible beneath you, and you can choose which you want to use.
- Try not to step too high, since this will put unnecessary strain on your arms
- The slightest shift in foot position can change your centre of balance and make a big difference to your stance on the rock.
- Use the tips and edges of the sole of your shoe to stand on holds, not your whole foot, nor stand with your arch

on a hold, since this will also throw out your balance.
- When **edging** (using small foot holds by applying the inner edge of the boot sole), be precise and stand hard on the holds, since a positive and confident approach is needed to make that millimetre of rubber stick to that credit-card edge. Get as much weight over the hold as possible. The more pressure the better.
- The same principle applies to **smearing** (climbing hold-less slabs by friction only). You need to get as much rubber in contact with the rock as possible, but keep an upright stance. A confident approach is needed on steep, smooth slabs.
- **Toe camming** can be used in rails and slots to pull the body round into certain positions. This can give you extra reach and also take some weight off your arms.

the outside edge of the foot is placed on a hold at or near hip-height. This brings that hip closer to the wall and allows for greater reach with the arm on that side.

THE FIGURE 4
This is an extreme technique that makes it possible to reach a high hold. One leg is placed over the forearm, which is used to lever the body higher. A good hand hold should be used, since a lot of strain is placed on the holding arm.

Different kinds of hand holds
EDGES
Any near horizontal, flat grip where you can put all, or some of your fingers. They can be incut, slightly sloping, or even rounded. It is important to feel for the best way to use the hold: don't just grab and pull; feel where you can get the best purchase with your fingers. The less purchase, the harder you will squeeze, which is directly related to getting pumped.

PRINCIPLES OF GOOD FOOTWORK

- Trust your shoes – they are designed for the job
- Stay relaxed and breathe evenly
- Take your time, never rush through a sequence, as this only brings on shoddy footwork and more strain on your arms
- Good footwork gets you further than strong arms

Edge

Crimp

Pocket

Jug

Undercling

Pinch grip

CRIMPERS

This is a tiny edge, where you can only use the tips of your fingers. The hold is so small, that when applying pressure, the middle knuckle bends at right angles, thereby forcing pressure directly down onto the finger tips. For added security, the thumb can also be brought up and wrapped over the index finger. This type of hold places enormous stress on the tendons running through your fingers and should be used with great care. Finger tape is often used to reinforce the tendons before attempting a crimpy route.

POCKETS

Any slot or hole in the rock into which you can put one or more fingers (usually only one or two) can be called a pocket. 'Sinker holes' can take two fingers up to the second knuckle. Sometimes pockets come as hideous, shallow indentations, where the tip of one finger can barely find purchase. For one-finger pockets, your first choice should always be the strong middle finger. If the pocket allows two fingers then the middle and ring finger should be used. To support the middle finger in a two-finger pocket, you have to choose between your ring finger and index finger. I generally find that my ring finger gives more stability to the hold. Pocket pulling puts severe stress on your tendons and joints. Most finger injuries come from this technique.

JUGS

If you can wrap your whole hand around a huge, positive hold, then you are clinging onto a jug or a bucket. The term is derived from 'jug handle'. Overhanging face climbing often consists of jug-hauling and can give immensely pleasurable climbing. However, don't underestimate the pump factor on these routes: they often feel easy to start with, and then carry on relentlessly, till your forearms start screaming.

UNDERCLINGS

Any hold that is used with the palm facing up is an undercling. They can range from the flat underside of a small roof to a great incut hold behind a flake. Mostly they are used with one hand to maintain balance while trying to gain height to reach holds with the other hand. However, underclinging a thin seam at the back of a roof, while your feet are smearing on the wall below, can be very taxing.

One of the most extreme and famous undercling pitches in the world is the Great Roof pitch on the Nose route on El Capitan in Yosemite Valley, as free-climbed by Lynn Hill.

PINCH GRIPS

The pinch grip sometimes offers the only way to overcome a troublesome section. It involves pinching a flange, rib, knob, or any type of protruding hold with finger and thumb. You should feel the hold first to determine the best place to grip. Smaller knobs are often best gripped with the thumb and side of the index finger.

SIDEPULLS

Climbers not only move upward, but also sideways. Any sideways move can feel a lot easier if a good sidepull is used. In face climbing sidepulls are used mainly to maintain balance while your legs are used for upward thrust. Any hold that is vertical, or near vertical, but cannot be used to pull down on, can be used as a sidepull.

SLOPERS

These grips are among the most dreaded for climbers, but some are worse than others. A sloper is a grip without a definite edge so that you cannot get a grip by simply latching on with the fingers. It can be a narrow edge, a flat sidepull, or a large, flat ledge-type grip that slopes down and outward. Either way they feel insecure. You should always feel around the sloper for a crease or ripple giving that little bit of extra purchase, which can make all the difference.

When using some slopers try using as much of your chalked-up palm as possible to get maximum friction on the rock.

GASTON

This can often create a strenuous stance for the climber, but on other occasions can offer the only way to stay in balance in a tenuous situation. This is when the best (most usable) part of the hold is on the side nearest you, so that instead of being able to pull on it, you have to push on it.

RAILS

These are horizontal cracks that can be anything from finger-width seams to huge, lovely incut edges. They can be found running along blank walls, but more commonly under roofs. They are often used to circumnavigate troublesome areas such as overhangs or blank sections to an easier break that can be climbed. Climbing along a rail can be called hand traversing or railing.

SUMMARY OF HAND HOLDS

When the most usable part of a hold is at the top it is usually named after its shape (sloper, edge or pocket). If the best part of a hole is on the side away from you, so that you can pull on it, it is called a sidepull or a layaway. If the best part of the hold is on the side nearest to you, so that you have to push on it, it is called a gaston (some people describe this as using a layaway with the wrong hand). If the best part of the hold is at the bottom it is called an undercling.

Sidepull

Sloper

Gaston

Rail

Resting

Being able to climb a steep route efficiently, keeping the pump (pain associated with muscle fatigue) in your arms at bay, and reaching the end of the pitch successfully and in control, is what climbing is all about. This demands not only good climbing skills, but also the ability to recognize rest spots and to use them effectively.

RULES OF RESTING

- Determine where you will rest before you even leave the ground. Visualize the pitch as chunks separated by rest spots. Climb the pitch with these rest spots imbedded in your mind. Use them when you reach them. The longer you climb the fitter you will get and the shrewder your eyes will become. Soon you will be using rests you always missed before – while your arms were screaming!
- Never pass up the chance to have a good rest. Even if you still feel fresh, take a minute to shake out your arms and relax your fingers – you never know how good the next rest spot will be, or how pumped you will get before reaching it.

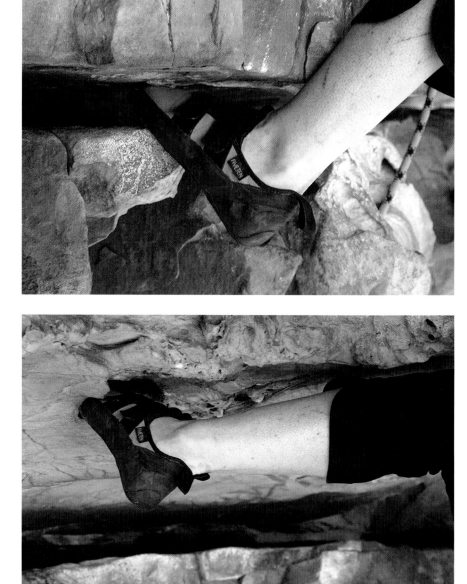

Top: 'Camming' a toe into a rail can prevent your feet from losing purchase.

Above: A 'toe cam' in a pocket under a roof can provide vital stability.

KINDS OF RESTS

- **Footwork.** Rests are not only gained by reaching something substantial to stand on. With creative footwork and body tension (tightening the abdominal muscles), rests can be devised in many different places. Even an overhanging wall can reveal good rests to the trained eye.
- **Handwork.** When climbing a face it is often possible to find a sidepull or an undercling hold off which to rest, provided your legs are taking most of your weight.
- **Prongs.** A prong is useful, since you can wrap your wrist or elbow around it to free your hands.
- **Stemming.** If you are climbing a corner, always look for solid

stemming positions. Even on overhanging corners and grooves you will often get a hands-off rest this way.

- **Knee bar.** This is when you jam the knee under a small roof by pushing up with the foot from a foot hold.

- **Jamming.** Jams are also extremely effective for resting, since you are relaxing the gripping muscles of your hands and using a different set of muscles to execute the jam. Be sure, though, that the jam is solid, since a precarious one will just pump you out more with the effort needed to keep it secure. When crack climbing, try jamming a whole arm or elbow into the crack to relieve the pressure on your hands or, better still, try wedging a knee, since this could give you that much sought-after hands-off rest.

- **Toe cams** and **heel hooks** are also used to take the weight off the arms. On a steep face, a toe cammed into a rail or hole can transfer a substantial amount of weight from the arms to the legs. A heel hook above the head when pulling through a roof can also offer a rest.

Above: Using a prong to rest. You can also wrap an arm around it to relieve pressure on the hands.

Above: Jams are good for resting tired hands and forearms. Here the climber shakes out one arm while jamming with the other.

Right: Rests are often gained by stemming. This climber has found a stemming rest on a steep corner.

Above: A rail can give you a short break to recuperate before tackling the rest of the pitch.

Top: *The climber, holding onto a rail, has both feet firmly on the rock, thus taking much weight off the arms.*

Above: *On a roof section the climber can rest the arms by hooking one foot onto a hold above the head.*

• **Just hanging there.** Obviously, the fitter you are the easier it is to rest and the more quickly you will recover. For example, a fit climber will be able to rest while hanging from a jug on an overhanging wall, simply by changing hands on the jug and giving the free hand a good shake out and a chance to recover. The muscles of an unfit climber need more time to rest and recover. Instead, the unfit climber will simply get more tired while hanging there – and finally fall off.

Above: The climber shakes out one hand, while holding onto a good grip with the other. It also gives the opportunity to study the next few moves of the route.

MAXIMIZING REST

Resting is all about freeing up one or both hands in order to regain the strength in your arms, so as to make it possible to continue and finish the pitch.

Whether you are standing on a ledge enjoying a hands-off rest, or hanging off a steep wall by a two-finger pocket, it is essential to 'shake out'. This is a technique used to maximize your time at a rest spot.

Let the resting hand hang free. Flex the fingers and the wrist. Shake your hand and forearm to allow the blood to move more quickly through the affected areas. Push your fingers against the rock or your leg, forcing them back in order to stretch the tendons in your fingers and forearms. Alternate hands. A warm glow in your forearms is a sign of good recovery, which means that you should start moving on. Remember, resting too long while hanging off your arms can also be detrimental.

Not all rests work for everybody. It depends on the climber's height, flexibility, strength and fitness. Often my partner gets a killer rest, which I slot into my memory bank, only to find when I get there that I can't use the same knee bar because my legs are too long. We all develop our skills slightly differently for climbing, and so, too, we learn and hone our resting skills according to our bodies. The more we climb the better we become.

ROPEWORK AND BELAYING

All you need to climb on rock is a pair of climbing shoes and a chalk bag. However, if this is all you have, you had better have a very strong head. Most people are under the impression that climbers use the rope and the various pieces of hardware to aid their ascent up rock walls. This is true for artificial (aid) climbing, but for free climbing, which constitutes about 95 per cent of all climbing worldwide, this is not the case. The climber uses hand and foot holds in the rock to make upward progress. The rope and all the other paraphernalia are only there to ensure that climbers do not plummet to their deaths in the event of a fall. But for the system to work effectively the climber needs to have more than a basic knowledge of the ropework and belay techniques involved. This kind of knowledge does not come overnight, but is absorbed slowly over a period of time through experience and application.

Knots

The main uses of knots in climbing are to tie into the rope, attach yourself to the anchor system, and to join ropes and cord. However, their one drawback is that they weaken the rope to some degree, depending on the knot and the rope. Ropes have knot strengths roughly proportional to their elasticity. The tighter and more acute the turns in a knot, the more it will affect the strength.

There are numerous knots that can be used in each situation, but on the following pages are the basic knots needed to be able to participate safely in the sport of climbing.

Right: Climbers ascending the limestone walls of the Verdon Gorge in France. These steep, pocketed routes are very 'exposed' – lots of fresh air under the climbers' feet.

TYING INTO THE ROPE

There are a number of ways to tie into the rope. The most common and trusted knot is the figure of eight. Another knot that is used to tie in is the bowline.

Figure of eight. Besides being the standard tie-in knot, the figure of eight is extensively used to connect to the anchor system; as a general knot to connect anything to the stance (haul bag or other paraphernalia); or to fix the rope to any piece of gear. It is easy to tie and has a distinctive shape (that of an eight) that will tell you at a glance if you have got it right or not. It can be tied in two different ways. The standard way for tying into the anchor system is on a bight, which can be tied anywhere in the rope by taking a loop. However, to tie the rope to your harness, or around any closed loop, you must use a **rewoven figure of eight**. This is the same, except that the knot is tied with a single strand of rope, threaded around the tie-on point and then rewoven to produce a standard figure of eight. In this case, it is usual to tie a stopper knot with the loose end to avoid any chance of the knot working loose. Another option is to feed the loose end back over and through the knot.

Figure of eight

▲ **1.** Form a bight of at least 250mm (10 in). Pass the bight behind the standing part in an anticlockwise underhand loop.

▲ **2.** Next, pass the bight in front of the standing part and again behind, ready to pass through the first loop formed.

▲ **3.** Bring the bight up through the loop and ensure that parallel parts do not cross over each other.

▲ **4.** Tighten the loop by pulling in opposite directions on the standing parts and the bight.

Tying a rewoven figure of eight to a harness

▲ **1.** Tie a single figure of eight and pass the working end through your harness loop and hold in your right hand.

▲ **2.** Pass the working end through your harness and start following the standing part back into the knot.

▲ **3.** Be sure to follow inside the line that exits the knot, so that the existing line remains on the outside of the finished knot.

▲ **4.** Ensure that the parts lie parallel to each other and that the working end has a tail long enough to tie a stop knot.

Tying a bowline to a harness

The bowline is not as not as easy to tie, or as common as the figure of eight, but is nevertheless used by many climbers. It is one of the original ways of tying into the rope. It tends to work itself loose, but is easier to untie after loading than the figure of eight. Always use a stopper knot on the loose end.

1. Pass the working end through your harness loop and hold it with your right hand.

2. Rotate your left palm down toward your heart to form a counterclockwise overhand loop with the standing part.

3. Reach up through the left-hand loop and pull a bight of the standing part down toward you through the loop.

4. Pass the working end through the bight from front to back, pulling through sufficiently to make the tail of the bowline loop, and hold the working end to itself.

5. Pull up on the standing part to pull the bight in the working end up through the first loop. The knot will twist to your left as you do this.

CONNECTING TO THE ANCHOR
Although the figure of eight knot is used as the standard anchor knot, the clove hitch is also used extensively, mainly in conjunction with the figure of eight, to tie into the anchor points.

The clove hitch makes life very easy when it comes to connecting to and equalizing your anchors on a stance. It can be tied anywhere in the rope and is fully and easily adjusted with little effort. Always pull the knot tight, since this is what makes it lock. A loose clove hitch can run very easily. A figure of eight knot must always be used as a back-up in a series of clove hitches at an anchor.

Clove hitch

1. Pass the line through the karabiner so that the loaded part is to your right.

2. Hold the left, free part of the line with your right hand, the back of the hand facing you, thumb down.

3. Twist the right hand clockwise to form an anti-clockwise overhand loop.

4. Slip the new loop through the karabiner gate, trapping the standing parts together with the crossing diagonal.

JOINING TWO ROPES

There are a number of reasons why one would want to join two ropes, the most common being so that you can abseil (rappel) further. Another reason would be for top-roping long pitches where a single rope, doubled, is not long enough. The ends of short pieces of rope can also be tied together to form rope slings.

The double fisherman's knot is the strongest way of tying two ropes together. After the knot is tied, a tail of about 8cm (3 in) should be left on either end. Once weighted, it can be very difficult to untie; make untying after an abseil easier by tying it with a reef knot in the middle. This allows the reef to take the main load with the double fisherman backing up in case of slippage.

The single fisherman's knot is similar to the double, but with only one turn on each side. Not as strong as its double version, the knot is seldom used, except for joining non-load-bearing cord.

Overhand knot. The one drawback of the double fisherman's knot is that it is quite bulky and can snag, or catch on a ledge, making it difficult to retrieve the rope after an abseil (rappel). If you are abseiling over rough slabs, or you feel that the chance of getting the knot snagged is higher than usual, then it would be better to use an overhand knot to join the ropes. The underside of the knot flattens out when the rope is pulled, lessening the chances of getting the knot caught. It is strong enough for abseiling, but it is not advisable for use in any other application.

Leave long ends.

Double fisherman's knot

▲ **1.** Lay the two lines beside each other, overlapping by about 350mm (14 in). Using the working end of the left line, bring it behind the standing part to tie a double overhand knot around the second line.

▲ **2.** Reverse the two lines and repeat step 1, so forming a second double overhand knot. If you cannot reverse the lines, tie the knot anticlockwise.

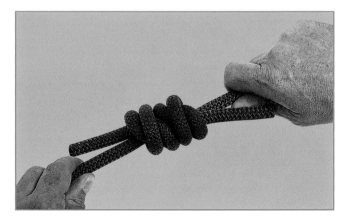

▲ **3.** Slide the two knots together, so that they mate and match. Fair the knot.

OTHER KNOTS

Tape Knot. Before tape slings could be bought ready-stitched and ready to use, climbers used to buy webbing off a reel and make their own slings. Although seldom done these days, you may occasionally need to tie the two ends of a piece of tape together. This knot works loose very easily, so it should be pulled as tight as possible and the tails should always be long and checked regularly.

Tape knot

▲ **1.** Tie an overhand knot in one end, leaving it loose.

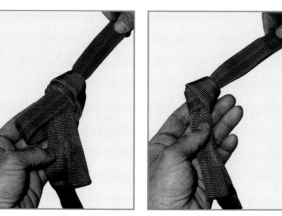

▲ **2.** The other end follows this overhand knot, but passing through in the opposite direction.

The alpine butterfly

The alpine butterfly is generally used to tie into the middle of the rope. It can be loaded from either end of the rope, or directly through the loop. It is relatively easy to untie after it has been weighted. The figure of eight is often used instead.

▲ **1.** Pass the working end of the line over your hand.

▲ **2.** Repeat so that you have three turns over and around the hand.

▲ **3.** Bring the entire inside loop over the other two, toward the fingertips.

▲ **4.** Bring the new inside loop over the other two again, so that the original middle loop is now over the first and third loops. Tuck this last loop back toward the thumb, but underneath the first two.

▲ **5.** Pull the middle loop out through the middle of the loops after sliding it off the hand. Fair the knot.

▲ **6.** Tighten by pulling firmly on each side.

The Prusik knot

Prusik knot. You should never embark on a multipitch route without your trusty set of prusik loops. They can be invaluable in an emergency: for instance, dangling in midair after a fall, with no way of getting back onto the rock. In a prusik knot the loop is attached to the main rope using a short sling of cord, preferably about 5mm in diameter. The loop is put behind the rope and then threaded through itself twice, then pulled tight. It is important to keep the knot symmetrical, because this way it bites deeper into the rope. The knot will slide up and down the rope if you push on the knot itself, but it will lock if the sling is pulled in either direction. With two prusik loops, one can ascend a rope with relative ease. (More about this under the section on prusiking.) Will not unlock under load.

▲ **1.** Open the prusik loop and place behind the line to which you are attaching the prusik.

▲ **2.** Pass the knotted end of the sling through its own open loop from front to back.

▲ **3.** Repeat step 2, ensuring that the passes do not cross each other and that they lie fair.

▲ **4.** After fairing, pull to ensure a snug fit.

▲ **5.** The knot holds by kinking the anchor line when loaded and relies on friction to hold after two turns. More turns will increase friction

▲ **6.** After clipping in your karabiner, you can loosen the knot by pushing it, unloaded, toward the anchor. Retighten by pulling the cord in the loaded direction.

The French Prusik knot (or autobloc)

The French prusik is similar to the prusik knot, but it can be released under tension, which is important in situations like escaping from the system (see emergency procedures p179).

◄ **1.** Pass the prusik loop around the anchor line with one round turn.

◄ **2.** Continue passing the knotted end around the line for three more round turns.

◄ **3.** Bring the knotted part of the loop down to meet the first part of the loop, so that you can pass a karabiner through both.

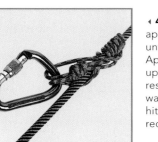

◄ **4.** Tighten the hitch by applying tension downward until it kinks the anchor line. Applying pressure to the upper turns of the hitch may result in it moving downward. This will allow the hitch to slide into the required location.

The Italian hitch (or Munter hitch)

The Italian hitch (or Munter hitch) is an invaluable knot that can be used to replace any belay or abseil device. It is one of the simplest knots to tie, yet extremely effective. If you have forgotten your belay device at home, or maybe dropped it halfway up a multipitch route, then the Italian hitch is your ticket out of an otherwise embarrassing pickle. Ideally it is used with a pear-shaped karabiner (not shown) and it is important to keep the running rope away from the gate of the karabiner.

▲ **1.** Make a loop by twisting so that (here) the end in your right hand passes over the end in your left hand.

▲ **2.** Form an overhand clockwise loop by gripping the line with the back of your hand toward you, and turn your hand so that the palm faces you.

▲ **3.** Pass the loop over the bill of the karabiner, trapping the loop against itself. Close the karabiner gate.

▲ **4.** Apply pressure to the inactive part to temporarily hold the line.

Belaying

Belaying is the act of holding or securing yourself, or your partner, by means of fixing the rope through a special device attached to your harness with a screw gate karabiner. In a typical situation, one climber is anchored to the stance and belays the other, who may be leading or following. Much thought must be given to setting up a belay stance as the anchors must always be arranged so as to accept the force generated on them in the direction of a potential fall. A standard belay should be able to withstand a downward and upward force and often also a sideways pull.

BELAY DEVICES

There are many different belay devices on the market.

In the early days, climbers (especially the leader), 'never fell'. This was because they had little protection gear and no belay system with which to hold a fall.

From the middle of the 20th century until the 1960s, climbers used body belays, where the rope was passed around the waist of the person belaying. In the event of a fall the friction caused by the rope running over the body would arrest the falling climber. Unfortunately, this would invariably cause a lot of pain and burn wounds to the belayer, as the rope would cut mercilessly into the flesh.

One of the first modern belay devices to make its appearance in

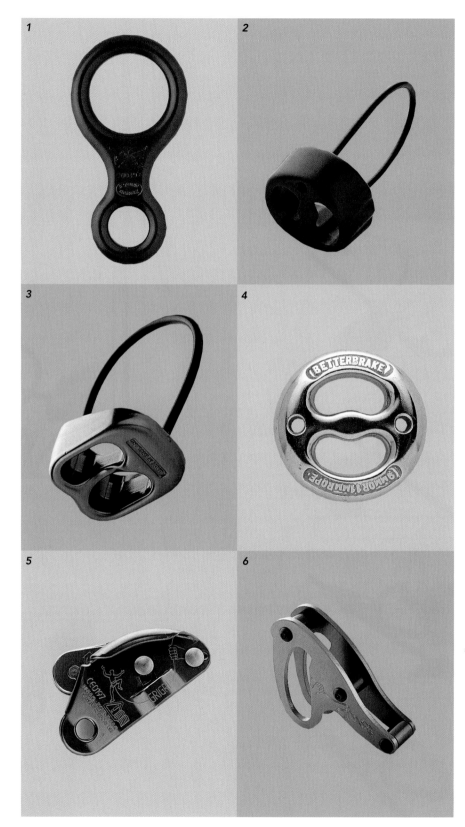

Above: *Belaying devices: 1) the figure eight, 2) Bug, 3) Variable Controller, 4) Betterbrake, 5) Gri Gri, 6) Single Rope Controller.*

Belay anchors

Cordelette equalizing all the anchor points

Anchor point attachment to harness

Belay device

Loose rope neatly flaked over belayer's feet

Rope to following climber

Above: A typical hanging belay.

the late 60s was the Sticht Plate. This was just a round aluminium plate with two slots for passing through the bight of one or two ropes. The bight would then be clipped to a screwgate karabiner on your harness, making a U-bend in the rope. In the event of a fall, the friction caused by the rope running through the plate would lock the system and arrest the fall. This worked amazingly well and also eliminated the painful process of letting the rope run across your body. It didn't take long before everybody was using it.

Since then, many new belay devices have hit the market from a variety of different manufacturers. Their designs differ slightly, but all work on the same principle as the original Sticht Plate.

However, belay devices, no matter how fancy, are not foolproof and it is important to keep your brake hand on the dead side of the rope. Grasping this side to stop the rope from sliding through the device is what arrests the fall. The rule is NEVER, no matter what the circumstances, to remove your brake hand from the rope.

Of course, one doesn't always get a nice flat ledge from which to belay, and one must improvise and adjust to what is offered by the rock and the particular climb on which you are. It could be a very cramped stance under a low roof, or a boulder jammed in a crack onto which you can only get one foot. Sometimes there is nothing at all. In this case the climber makes a hanging stance, secured by equipment and hanging on this with full body weight.

Manufacturers are always inventing new devices and bits of gear to make life easier on the vertical plane. About 12 years ago a French company came up with a new belay device that was totally different from all the rest. This was the Gri Gri. This device has a movable camming action which closes the gap through which the rope runs, when the rope runs at a sudden high speed – very much like the action of a car seat belt. Although the Gri Gri should lock without fail with every fall, it is still prudent to keep your brake hand on the rope (as stated in the instruction booklet that comes with it) and some training is required before use.

The camming action is rather sensitive, making paying out rope to the leader tricky if you are not used to the device. Also, because the device has such a good reputation for being self-locking, many people tend to neglect the golden rule of always keeping the brake hand on the rope. This is particularly dangerous when lowering someone off a sport route.

When lowering, the belayer pulls a lever back to release the tension on the cam and so frees the rope, allowing it to run. At this stage the Gri Gri is, in principle, like any other standard belay

Above: The Gri Gri is an auto-locking belay device mainly used in sport climbing.

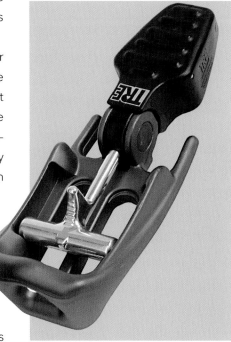

Above: The Tré is a very effective auto-locking device, but fiddly to operate.

Above: The Reverso is a cleverly designed device that can be used as a regular belay plate or as an auto-locking device.

device and if the brake hand is not holding the rope firmly, the climber being lowered will plummet earthward. Created for sport climbing, the Gri Gri was designed to be used with one rope and only ropes with diameters of between 10mm and 11mm.

Over the past few years a number of other locking and semi-locking belay devices have been introduced to the market. They are smaller and lighter than the Gri Gri and most take double ropes, making them suitable for traditional climbing. Unfortunately, few are without drawbacks. The Reverso, for instance, is nigh-on impossible to release while under tension from a dangling climber. The Tré, on the other hand, is fiddly to attach to your harness belay loop and its design is such that it is easy for the climber to make an error.

One very handy knot to know is the Italian (or Munter) hitch. It can be used to perform a very effective belay and is in fact widely used as a first choice by many climbers in Europe. Knowing this hitch will save you if you accidentally drop your belay device on pitch five of a ten-pitch route. (See p81).

Left: *Belaying on Torres del Paine in Patagonia.*

Communication

On single pitch or short multipitch routes, where climbers are visible to each other, a few abbreviated calls or improvised hand signals should be sufficient, but add a few variables to the equation and an unambiguous system of communication is vital.

All calls should be delivered in a loud and clear voice and in the direction of the person to whom you are calling. You could be shouting at someone 50m (164ft) away, with a rock buttress between yourselves. There could also be other noise interference like a strong wind or crashing waves on a sea cliff. In a gorge you may have to contend with an echo. In this case speak slowly and let each word be heard in turn.

Always be attentive to the situation so that you can answer promptly. On a route where calls could be difficult to hear because of wind, for instance, devise a system of rope-tug signals to facilitate communication. These should not be complex, but a simple, foolproof system. An experienced climber will know the order in which calls are used during a pitch and rope tugs can easily be used in place of calls.

Above: Communication is easy when within sight of each other, but wind carries away sound and climbers often lose visual contact.

CLIMBING CALLS

A system of calls has been developed which is now standard throughout the English-speaking world.

On belay! (or Safe!) (the climber is safely on belay.) Normally used together with the call that follows.

Climb when ready!

Climbing! (when about to start climbing.) The second's reply to the leader.

Climb! Leader confirms that the second can start climbing.

Take in! Usually from the person climbing, to ask belayer to take up slack in the rope. Also used on the stance to tell the leader to take up the remaining slack in the rope before starting to climb.

Slack! When the rope is held too tight and either the leader or second needs more rope.

Off belay! (leader is safe on a stance.) Leader's call to the second.

Off belay ! (rope has been removed from the belay device.) The second's reply.

That's me! (all the slack rope on the stance has been taken up and is pulling tight on the second.) The second's call to the leader.

Tight rope! (the second needs assistance from the rope on a difficult section.) Only to be used if the rope is above the climber.

Watch me! (pay careful attention during a particularly difficult section.) From climber to belayer.

Take! When the climber wants to rest on the rope.

Lower! The climber wants to be lowered to the ground or stance.

Below! (in an urgent voice.) Rock (or equipment) has been dislodged by the climber and is falling earthward. Also used when throwing a rope down for abseiling, i.e. 'Rope below!'

Placing and removing protection gear

The sport of rock climbing is so 'equipment reliant' that without our hi tech gear it would be a sport only for the brave or insensate.

The equipment by itself does not guarantee safety, however. Without the knowledge to use it correctly, you are climbing with a false sense of security.

Protection gear – springloaded camming devices (SLCDs), wire nuts, hexcentric nuts and slings, for instance – is used to anchor yourself to the rock on stances between pitches. It also protects the leader, in the event of a fall while climbing a pitch.

Getting the placement of your gear right is vital to your own safety and that of the whole party. With practice you will slowly develop confidence. Your gear placement can only be as good as the rock it is placed in, however, so always check the quality of the rock when placing gear. A nut wedged behind an expanding flake could be dangerous: besides the possibility of the nut ripping from its tenuous housing, there is also the chance of the flake being dislodged. Not only will you then have to contend with a fall, but also a deadly missile plummeting toward you or your belayer.

Never try to find a crack or slot that will take a specific size or piece of gear. The chances of finding the perfect crack for your no. 2

cam, which you are clutching and holding up like a lamp in the dead of night, are extremely slim. Rather look for a piece of gear that will fit the crack.

The leader sets off on an average rock pitch carrying a standard set of gear. This would include a selection of 8–12 SLCDs in a range of sizes from tiny (no. 00) to medium/large (nos. 2–3) and sometimes bigger; a selection of 12–16 wire nuts, also in a range of sizes; a few larger hexcentric nuts; and a handful of slings.

With this selection of gear you can take on most rock pitches. As cracks, rails and slots present themselves on your way up a pitch, you inspect each to determine what type of gear, and which size, would be most suitable. Select a piece and place it. If it isn't spot-on, try the next size up or down. Not all cracks are gear-friendly and some are worse than others due to their shape and rugosities, or bumps, on the inside. In these cases one has to inspect the crack carefully to determine the best possible place to insert the piece of gear.

SLINGS

Slings were the first pieces of gear used by climbers to protect themselves. They are also the easiest to place. They are used to sling horns (spikes of rock), or to wrap around bollards, often giving solid protection. Careful inspection can also reveal touch points in rails, or threadable pockets.

Removal. Slings are generally the easiest gear to remove. Carefully free any jammed areas and lift it off, or slide it out of its placement.

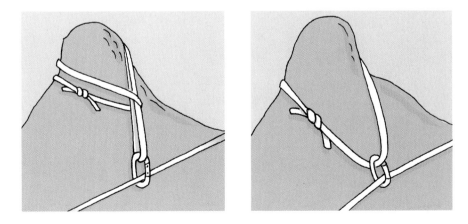

Above: Slings can be used in many different ways. The illustration on the left shows a sling girthed to a prong. This is used when there is a chance that the sling can be lifted accidentally from the prong. The illustration on the right shows a sling simply looped over a prong. This can be used when there is little chance of the sling been lifted.

WIRED NUTS

Wired nuts have been around for a long time and have evolved greatly in design and shape over the past ten years or so. They come in a range of sizes from tiny micronuts for thin seams to chunky stoppers for use in much wider cracks. Wires (or nuts as they are more commonly known) come in curved and fluted shapes for greater ease of placement and for better seating when placed. When placing nuts, always look for constrictions within the crack, behind which the nut can be wedged. Choosing the correct size for a particular crack or slot is vital: although a no. 5 might fit well (90%) and feel good, a no. 4 could slot in even deeper and give you a 98% placement. Or the no. 4 feels just a tad loose and might be in danger of being pulled through, while a no. 5 might fit snug and tight. Turning the nut on its side can also improve the fit.

The nut must be fiddled into the crack, but beware of deep placements, since this often makes it difficult to remove the nut. After placing the nut, always give it a few solid tugs, so that the nut head gets seated well within its housing, which will greatly reduce the risk of the nut being lifted out by the drag of the rope.

Always place nuts in such a way that the force generated by a fall will seat the nut further.

Removal. Because nuts are seated tightly, they often need a

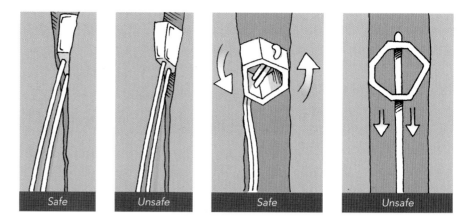

Above: *Wires should be placed so the rock on either side grips evenly across the whole body of he nut. The correct size is vital for a solid fit.*

Below: *Hexcentric nuts are designed in such a way that when placed correctly in a parallel-sided crack, the force generated by a fall will cam the unit in tighter.*

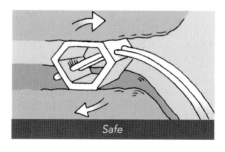

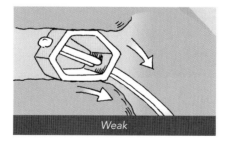

good yank in the opposite direction to release them. Use a sling, or quick-draw attached to the cable of the nut for grip and leverage. In most cases this works like a charm, but there will always be the odd stubborn nut that

feels it is too early to leave the party. For these cases, a nifty little device, called a nut remover, comes into play. It is simply a flattened metal rod 15–20cm (6–8 in) long, which can be inserted into the crack and placed against the offending nut. One sharp knock with the heel of the hand should loosen the nut.

HEXCENTRIC NUTS

Hexcentrics are six-sided nuts with each face a different size so that they can be used in parallel-sided cracks (apart from their use as conventional nuts to jam behind constrictions in cracks). The beauty about hexcentrics is that they also come in very large sizes, up to a no. 11, the size of a large fist. These can be useful in large, uneven cracks, where nothing else will work.

Removal. The smaller sizes can be removed like any wired nut, while the larger ones can be grasped with your fingers, or hand, making removal much easier.

CAMMING UNITS

Cams were developed in the 1970s for the smooth, parallel-sided cracks of Yosemite Valley, California, USA. Although not accepted immediately, cams soon became standard gear on everyone's rack and proved invaluable in all types of climbing.

How cams work. All cams have three or four cam wheels which can be contracted by pulling a trigger mechanism on the shaft. It is then placed into a crack where the trigger is released, causing the cam wheels to expand outward against the side of the crack. Any outward force on the shaft (caused by a fall) will generate an outward force through the cam wheels, which will keep the cam in place.

Cams can be placed in almost any crack, although it is not as easy as just shoving them in. It takes a fair amount of practice. Cams work best if the crack is smooth and parallel-sided; in these cases they are also relatively easy to place. The size of the cam is important because cam wheels are strongest in the middle 50% of their movement range. A cam that is holding with the last 5 or 10% of its expansion range (almost completely open), is weak and at risk of being wrenched from its housing. At the other extreme, when a cam's wheels are completely contracted there is no room for sufficient expansion to enable it to grip adequately. The other (rather expensive) downside of this is that it makes the cam impossible to remove, since one needs to depress the cam wheels to be able to extract the device.

When placing a cam, look carefully at the surfaces of the crack into which the cam wheels are going to bite. Ideally, the sides of the wheels need to get in contact with as much surface area as possible and be placed in the most parallel part of the crack. Sometimes, turning the cam around helps with better seating. Be aware of inward flaring cracks. They are difficult to spot and can render your cam useless if it slips into the open flare.

Cams sometimes have a tendency to 'walk' into cracks. This happens when the rope moves from side to side, making the cam creep inward. This can be avoided by placing an extension sling on the cam.

Right: It is important to get a cam placement right to be able to utilize its full potential. The placement top left is perfect, with a good 25 per cent range of movement on either side of the set cams. The one adjacent to it is overcammed. This placement is weak, since there is no give between the cam wheels. The placement shown in the centre illustration is also very weak since the cam has almost no room to expand inside the crack. The cam on the right should be placed at more of a downward angle, so that the force of a fall won't wrench the unit.

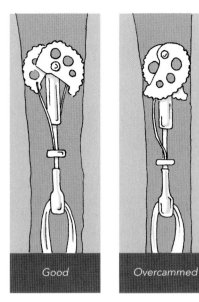

Good   Overcammed

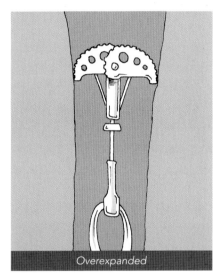

Overexpanded

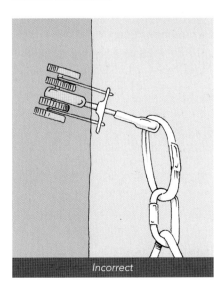

Incorrect

Removal. Cams should always be removed with great care, since a sudden movement in the wrong direction can permanently jam the unit. Carefully inspect the placement, and check out a likely removal path. Grab the shaft and firmly squeeze the trigger, loosening the cam inside the crack. Now carefully move the cam along the removal path until it is free. Sometimes you might have to alter the removal path, depending on the shape of the crack. Avoid pushing the cam deeper than its original placement.

If the cam has 'walked', or a nervous leader has stuffed the cam so deep that you cannot reach the trigger with your fingers, then reach for your trusty nut remover. A good nut remover will have two little claws on one end. Insert the shaft of the nut remover into the crack and latch the claws over the trigger. Press the shaft with your thumb and you should feel the cams releasing. Gingerly work the unit toward you until you can grab it with your hand.

Right: When a badly-placed cam has jammed into the rock, a nut remover can be used to release individual cams. It can also be used to reach the trigger of a cam placed too deeply.

TRI-CAMS

Tri-Cams are not as widely used as wired nuts and camming units, but work well in shallow rails and pockets, where nothing else will fit. They have a curved face on the one side, and a wedge-shaped knob on the other. They are placed with the tape sling running over the top of the curved side, so that when loaded the piece is pulled into a cammed position 'increasing' its size to hold it in place.

Removal. Tri-Cams are simple to remove, since they are always in a shallow placement, with little or no constriction.

SPECIAL PLACEMENTS

Now and then you are faced with a situation that demands creative gear placement. This sometimes happens when you need a particular size of nut that you have already used earlier on the pitch, or the cracks are the wrong angle to get the right directional pull.

Two nuts together. Try using two nuts together (one upside down) in a crack. As force is applied to the one nut, it will exert a force onto the other one, thereby creating a double jammed nut.

Opposed nuts. Sometimes it is necessary to use two connected nuts pulling in opposite directions, so that they hold each other in place. This is done with a sling between the two nuts (or cams) and one clip-in point. Make sure that there is no slack in the system.

Removal. Apply the same principles as when removing single pieces of the same gear.

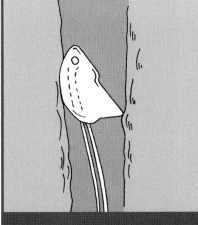

A well-placed tri-cam will cam solidly into the crack when loaded.

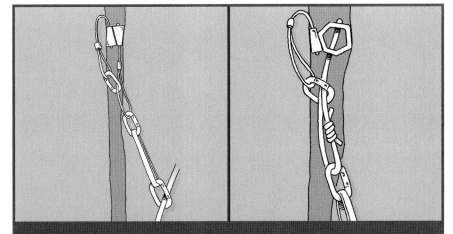

When placing two nuts together, make sure that the faces of the nuts fit well together in the crack where they are placed.

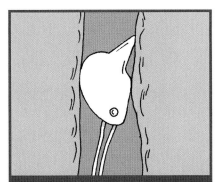

A poorly placed tri-cam will not have much holding strength when loaded. This placement will rely more on the constriction of the crack for stability.

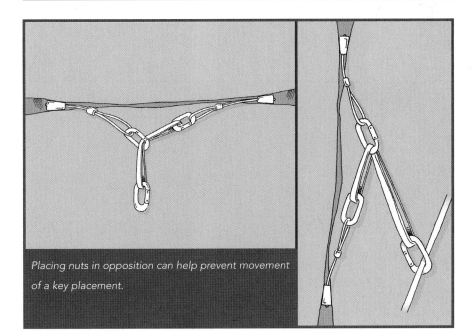

Placing nuts in opposition can help prevent movement of a key placement.

PITONS

Today, pitons are rarely used for protection on a traditional free climb, but still have an important place in the world of big wall and aid climbing. Pitons (also called pegs, or pins) come in different shapes and sizes and are selected from your rack to fit into various cracks. They are pounded in with a hammer up to the hilt, which has an eye for clipping. Any piton that is not sunk up to the hilt should be tied off on the shaft as close to the rock as possible to avoid unnecessary leverage.

When banging in a piton, a good high-pitched ringing tone denotes a good placement in sound rock. A dull, hollow sound, on the other hand, means a bad placement in less than perfect rock.

Removal. Generally, all pitons are removed by bashing them from side to side until they loosen enough to be pulled out by hand.

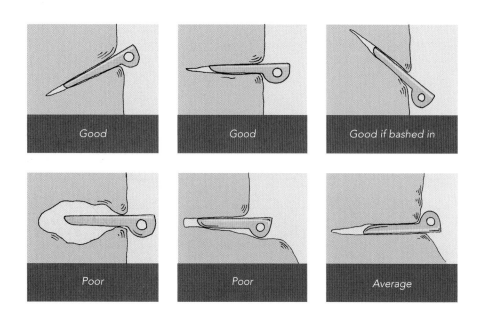

Above: *Various piton placements showing poor, average and good placements.*

Below: *A selection of pitons.*

GEAR REMOVAL TIPS

In many cases it can be more tiring to remove a piece of gear than climbing the pitch, but you can make it easier for yourself.

- Try to get into a comfortable, relaxed position before starting to remove gear.
- Get in line with your gear before attempting any removal procedure. It makes life much easier to be able to see the piece of gear you are removing, rather than fiddling with something above your head, not sure of which way to shift it.
- Remove gear by reversing the order in which it was placed: if it was slotted down and behind a constriction, then remove it by pushing it back and up.
- Impatient tugging and pulling may only set the gear more solidly, when a careful tap or wiggle will do the trick.

Route descriptions and Reading the rock

Throughout the world, most climbing areas and routes have been documented. This is done for two reasons: so that records can be kept for historical purposes; and so that other climbers can visit these areas and enjoy the climbs.

Route guides help climbers find the area, the crag and then the climb they want to do, with a description of the route to follow. It includes useful tips like weather patterns and what special gear is needed. However, it is often not as simple as that.

Following a bolted route (single or multipitch), is normally straightforward, because there is a line of shiny bolts to link the route. However, a traditional route (especially a multipitch climb in a remote setting) requires good mountain experience in addition to a good route guide.

A rock wall is often riddled with different features: corners, arêtes, cracks, chimneys, overhangs, rails, ledges and other formations. A rock climb follows and links up different features as it snakes its way up the wall.

ROUTEFINDING

Typically, you find yourself, for instance, at the foot of a 200m (666ft) wall. It is your first visit to the area and you are clutching a route description of one of the classic routes first climbed in the 1950s. The wall is about 300m (980ft) wide and has a complex series of cracks, corners and overhangs. Where do you start?

- Your first step is to find the start of the route. It will help if you can find the start of any route up the wall. Often route descriptions use other routes as reference points ('Start 10m to the left of Lounge Lizard', for instance).
- Look at the whole first pitch and see if the route description fits where you think the pitch goes. Avoid forcing the route description to match the pitch. It is

Top left: If the climb appears more difficult than the published grade, then you may be looking at the wrong route or even the wrong crag.

ROUTE-FINDING TIPS

- A traditional route almost always follows a natural line so that protection can be placed.
- When checking out the line of your route on a wall, remember the grade of the climb. An easy route is unlikely to take a flared overhanging crack line. So if your (visual) line meets up with such a feature, you may well have made an error somewhere lower down. Retrace and try to find a way around it.
- Check the year the route was first climbed. A climb that was opened in the 1950s means that limited gear was available to protect the route. If you are checking a bold looking pitch, ask yourself: 'Is it likely that this pitch could be climbed over 50 years ago?' Also check who made the first ascent: some climbers from the golden era have very bold reputations. Using this knowledge, and some common sense, you should be able to work out roughly where the route goes.

remarkably easy to convince yourself that a shallow corner is actually a deep recess, or even that a shrub is a tree.

- Once you are confident that you have found the start, step back a bit and examine the whole wall. Start at your first pitch and then link up pitch after pitch according to your route description until you top out.

Written route descriptions are normally one person's interpretation of a route, whether single or multipitch. Some people are meticulous in their descriptions, leaving almost no room for error, while others can be exceptionally slap-dash, often omitting important information like a traverse to the left or right that links features together. Everybody sees things through different eyes and will explain any given route in a different fashion.

A route description should be taken only as a rough guide. Reading the rock and relying on sound mountain experience is vital if you are to find your way up most multipitch climbs.

A different way of describing climbs is by a topographical diagram, or 'topo'. This is simply a sketch of a route using a set of recognized symbols to convey the information needed to follow the route.

All written route descriptions and topo drawings contain jargon and symbols that are unique to the sport of climbing and continuous use will build up the experience

you need to fully understand them. It is wise to go with an experienced climber when attempting your first multipitch climb.

CELESTIAL JOURNEY   140M   22   ★★★

Start: At a boulder below the smooth grey groove 25m (82ft) up.

P1: 35m (115ft) 22* From the boulder, climb the crack and follow the groove to a ledge on the right.

P2: 15m (50ft) 20 Climb the groove and corner above to a large ledge.

P3: 30m (100ft) 22 Climb the smooth grey face until a rail at 10m (33ft) enables one to move 3m (10ft) left to a peg and up to a small ledge. Continue to another ledge. Belay across to the left.

P4: 10m (33ft) 19 Step left and climb the grey wall past a peg to a big ledge. Scramble up and right to the groove in the orange wall.

P5: 20m (66ft) 21 Climb the left-facing off-width and crack to a big ledge.

P6: 30m (100ft) 20 Climb the crack above past a block to a groove which leads up to a hole. Rail 3m (10ft) left then go up and left to a ledge and the top.

*These figures denote the grade, which differs from counry to country.

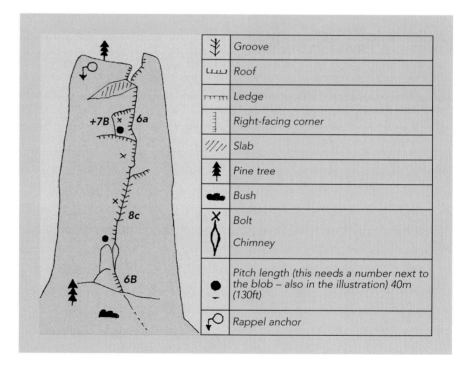

⬇	Groove
⌐⎵⌐	Roof
⊓⊓⊓	Ledge
⌐	Right-facing corner
/////	Slab
▲	Pine tree
🌿	Bush
✕	Bolt
◇	Chimney
●	Pitch length (this needs a number next to the blob – also in the illustration) 40m (130ft)
⌐○	Rappel anchor

Top: An example of a typical route description.

Above: An example of a typical topo (topographical) diagram.

Abseiling (rappelling)

Contrary to what most people imagine, abseiling is not something that is done for a cheap thrill, or an adrenaline rush. In mountaineering and climbing, abseiling is used only as a means of descent, to retreat off a route, or to access the start of a climb and should be used only when there is no other alternative.

Ask any climber and they will tell you that abseiling is the most dangerous part of the climbing game and wise mountaineers have a healthy respect for it.

WHAT IS ABSEILING

Abseiling (also known as rappelling) is simply the act of sliding down a rope using a friction device attached to your climbing harness. It is done in a controlled manner with the brake hand regulating your speed.

WHY IS ABSEILING SO DANGEROUS?

Abseiling in a commercial situation, where big steel bolts are used as an anchor, is safe. There is a staff of trained personnel to look after clients, who are attached to a second safety rope. But this is not mountaineering.

Mountaineers are responsible for their own anchor points. Setting up a sound anchor point with traditional gear takes experience and should only be attempted when totally confident with gear placement. If the anchor were to pull

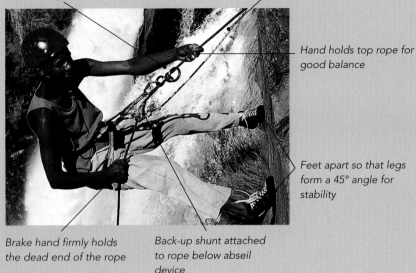

Figure of eight abseil device attached to harness belay loop with screwgate karabiner

Safety top rope, (the climber is being belayed from above)

Hand holds top rope for good balance

Feet apart so that legs form a 45° angle for stability

Brake hand firmly holds the dead end of the rope

Back-up shunt attached to rope below abseil device

Above: *A good abseil position, with the novice climber backed up by a shunt and a safety rope, being belayed from above, while he learns and acquires confidence.*

out, there would be no back up: you would be in for the long ride.

Each anchor is made up of several anchor points, all equalized, so that the force exerted on each is more or less the same.

If you are on top of a crag and need to access the base, you may have a wide variety of anchor points to choose from, making the abseil a fairly safe proposition. At the other extreme, you can find yourself on a little stance in the middle of a 200m (656ft) wall. There you are: three pitches up a climb when the weather takes a turn for the worse and you decide that it is a good idea to retreat.

Now you are faced with one or two square metres (yards) of rock

to set up your anchor, knowing that any gear placed will have to be left behind. Do not skimp on gear for your anchor point. I know that a cam is very expensive, but it will be of no use to you when you lie smashed up on the scree below. Make those anchors as solid as possible. Place as many different pieces of gear as you deem necessary.

Once you have a solid anchor point or, better still, your chosen line of descent is equipped with double-bolt stations, you still have no reason to relax and drop your guard. Before sliding over the edge, make sure that:

• your harness is fastened properly and fits snugly around your waist

- the rope is attached properly and running smoothly through the abseil device, which is connected to your harness belay loop with a locking karabiner
- the rope reaches the ground, or the next abseil station. If in any doubt, tie a knot in the end of the rope to avoid sliding straight off the end.

As you slide over the edge, make sure that you keep your hand firmly on the rope that runs from your waist down to the ground. This is your brake hand and is used to control your speed and, if gripped tightly enough, will stop you altogether. If this hand lets go, then you will free-fall all the way to the bottom.

THE METHOD OF ABSEILING

Inexperienced abseilers find it awkward and often scary to get started on an abseil. The initial kick-off is easier if the anchor point is above your head. The lower the anchor point, the more awkward it will be to set off. Once you have your weight firmly on the rope, spread your legs about 45° apart. This will stop you from swinging from side to side. Slowly let the rope slide through your hands and through the abseil device, keeping your knees slightly bent and allowing your body to assume a 45° angle to the rock. If your body is too upright, your feet will skid off and you will swing in toward the rock. When this happens, fight the instinct

Figure eight abseil device, attached to harness with screwgate karabiner

Prusik loop as back-up

Screwgate karabiner

Brake hand firmly on rope to control the speed

Feet pushing body out from the rock.

Above: *A good abseil position – the climber supports himself with his legs, controlling hand in position, knees slightly bent and body at a 45° angle to the rock.*

(disastrous in this case) to bring up your hands to protect your face as you swing in to hit the rock. In the process, you would let go of the rope with dire results.

Once in a comfortable, 45° position, start walking backward down the wall. Always keep your full bodyweight on the rope, even when crossing ledges on your way down. Taking your weight off the rope reduces the stretch and could even allow a little slack, so that when resuming the abseil after the ledge, you will drop until the slack and stretch is taken up. This will

give you a start, and you might release the rope as a result.

When you reach the ground release the ropes from your abseil device and shout clearly up to your partner: 'ROPE FREE!' This indicates that you are finished and that the next person can start abseiling. If it is a hanging abseil station, make sure that you are clipped in properly to the anchors before releasing the rope.

In windy conditions keep the rope coiled around the body or stacked in a rope bag. Coils can then be released while abseiling.

Top: A prusik loop can be used as a back-up on the abseil rope.

Above: If the rope leading to the ground is pulled firmly, the abseiler will be stopped immediately. This is a good safety back-up for beginners.

BACK-UPS

Because of the unforgiving nature of abseiling, beginners should have some form of back-up in place until they are comfortable with the practice. Some people, no matter how experienced, always use a back-up while abseiling, others only for the first few abseils. There are a several standard back-ups:

1. Safety rope from above. A separate safety rope is attached to the harness of the abseiler, who is then belayed by someone from above. If the abseiler lets go of the rope, the belay rope will catch the fall. The disadvantage of this system is that it is time-consuming.

2. Prusik loop. This is a simple, yet effective way of backing up, also used by experienced abseilers. Take a short prusik loop and attach it to the rope underneath the abseil device, using a prusik knot (see p80). Then clip the loose end into a locking karabiner attached to your leg loop. While abseiling, keep the knot in your hand and slide it down as you descend. If you happen to let go of the rope, the knot will lock and you will stop immediately. The prusik loop shouldn't be too long.

3. Holding the rope from below. This system is used when experienced abseilers find themselves abseiling with a relative beginner, but there is no second rope or prusik loop to use as a back-up. Connect the rope to the beginner's abseil device, then connect yourself beneath the beginner's abseil device. You abseil first, leaving the beginner behind. Once you have reached the safety of the ground (or the next stance), pick up the ends of the ropes and shout up for the beginner to start abseiling. Keep a firm grip on the ends of the ropes, but leave some slack. If the ropes are pulled taut from below, it will stop the abseiler in mid-stride.

4. Back-up anchor. When abseiling from less than perfect anchors, add a back-up anchor that is only removed by the last man down.

Above: Tuck away loose clothing and tie long hair out of the way. If caught in your abseil device it will lock solid.

JAMMING THE ABSEIL DEVICE

Anything getting stuck in the abseil device will jam up the system immediately and, unless experienced and prepared, you will probably need to be rescued even though you may be only 2–3m (7–10ft) off the ground.

The most common cause of jammed-up abseils is loose clothing, so keep it tucked away. Hair that is pulled into the abseil device will not only jam it, but it is also extremely painful. Always keep long hair tied back, or tucked up under your helmet. Even body hair like chest hair can be pulled into the device. Always check that there is nothing that can threaten the smooth running of the system.

If something gets stuck in your abseil device, the simplest way would be to attach a (long) prusik loop to the rope above the device. Then stand up in the loop, taking your weight off the abseil device. This will allow you to clear the jam and resume abseiling. If you don't have a prusik loop, try improvising with a sling, otherwise you will probably need to be rescued, which is highly embarrassing in this sort of situation.

PULLING THE ROPES

Once you have reached the ground safe and sound, the ride is not yet over. You still have to retrieve your ropes – which are notorious for getting stuck. Ensuring a trouble-free retrieval starts with the way you set up your anchor point.

- Make sure that the rope is running around a single bend. Never run a rope around more than one bend. This puts unsafe and unnecessary strains on the anchor, and will create a huge amount of friction, making it impossible to pull the ropes.
- If you have joined two ropes together, always place the knot in a position where it won't get snagged on the edge of a ledge or in a groove near the anchor.
- While abseiling, keep the ropes from twisting. It is much easier to pull ropes that are running without twists in them.
- Once the first person has reached the end of the abseil, it is important to do a quick check to see if the ropes run freely. If there is a problem, it is easier to rectify the situation with someone still on top.
- Once you start pulling the ropes, try to keep them running continuously, rather than jerk them in a stop-start fashion. A smooth pull will reduce the chances of the knot getting caught anywhere.
- When nearing the end of the rope, try to pull the rope away from the face. Give the rope a solid outward tug just as you judge the end of the rope to be leaving the top anchor point. This allows the rope to fall clear of the face and prevents the rope from getting snagged on vegetation or jammed in cracks.

The importance of keeping your ropes running well and free of snags and jams will be brought home to you when your ropes jam on the third abseil of a six-abseil descent off a peak – especially if the light is failing, or the weather threatening. This often leads to frustration, anger and very scary practices to retrieve ropes.

Step 1

Above: *Prusiking is a simple, yet effective way of ascending a rope. On the left the climber has slid up his foot sling and is about to stand up. On the right the climber has stood up and is adjusting the prusik loop attached to his harness so that he can sit down and slide his foot sling up again*

Prusiking/Jumaring

There you are three pitches up, feeling quite lonely on your little stance. You lean out and crane your neck to see where the leader is. Your eye scans the rock, high above the overhanging crack, further up and over to the right above the big roof to a semi-hanging stance where you can just make out the leader sorting out the belay. All too soon comes the cry 'Cliiiiimb when reeaadyyyyy!'

You set out nervously, the crack pushes you out as you crank through the crux jamming section. You get through that and onto the headwall. 'Jeez, this is still quite steep,' you think to yourself as you start the long traverse across the lip of the big roof. You can't help but notice that the gear is rather spaced and, silently cursing the leader, you try to stay as calm as possible.

Then comes the awkward reach across that dreaded blank section. You set yourself up, stand on the tiny toe hold and stretch for the good hold. Next thing you know you're feeling the air whistling through your helmet as you pendulum into space. A few minutes later you are spinning on the end of your rope with 100m (330ft) of crisp mountain air sucking at your bowels.

What happens now? With no way of getting back onto the rock you can be faced with a serious dilemma. You can't be lowered to the ground, and the leader certainly can't hoist you up to the lip of the overhang. What do you do? If you have a set of prusik loops clipped to the back of your harness (for those 'just in case' situations), you can pop them on the rope and 'jug' up a few metres till you can step back on the rock and carry on climbing.

1. Make yourself a pair of prusik loops from some 5mm cord – One long (about 95cm; 37 in) and one short (about 47.5cm; 19 in). This is not the length of the cord, but the length of the knotted and finished loop. Use a double fisherman's knot to tie the ends (see p78). The lengths of the prusik loops depend on your height. The measurements given here are for a person about 1.75m to 1.83m (5ft 9 in to 6ft) tall. Attach these loops to the back of your harness and forget about them. They weigh nothing and you may never need them, but in the event of a fresh-air wallow, they are invaluable. If you do need to fire up the old prusik loops, then read on.

2. Remove the prusik loops from your harness. Attach the long one to the rope first, using a prusik knot (see p80). This is for your foot. Then attach the short one, for your harness, above the long one.

3. With both prusik loops attached to the rope in front of you, put one foot (whichever one you favour) into the foot loop, but before you stand on that foot, slide the knot up the rope as far as your foot can comfortably reach, then stand up using your hands on the rope above to keep your balance.

4. While standing in your foot loop, use one hand to grab the knot of the waist loop and slide that up till it can go no further and then simply sit down in your harness.

5. Repeat the process as many times as necessary to get you back onto the rock. Once the knots have been weighted they can become a bit tight on the rope. To loosen them just push the upright part back to unlock the knot.

6. Once back on solid rock and standing reasonably comfortably, remove the prusik loops and carry on climbing.

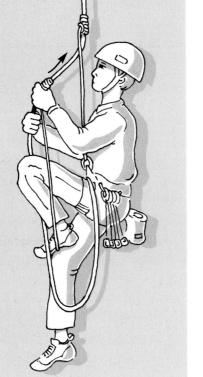

1. *With one foot in the loop, slide the knot as high as your foot can reach.*

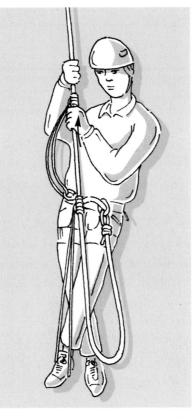

2. *Stand up in the foot loop, and slide the waist loop knot as far up as it will go.*

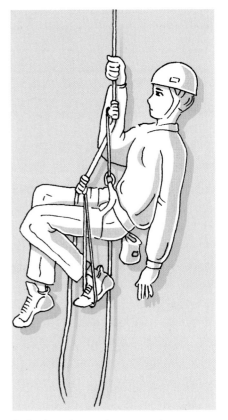

3. *Sit down in your harness and prepare to repeat the process.*

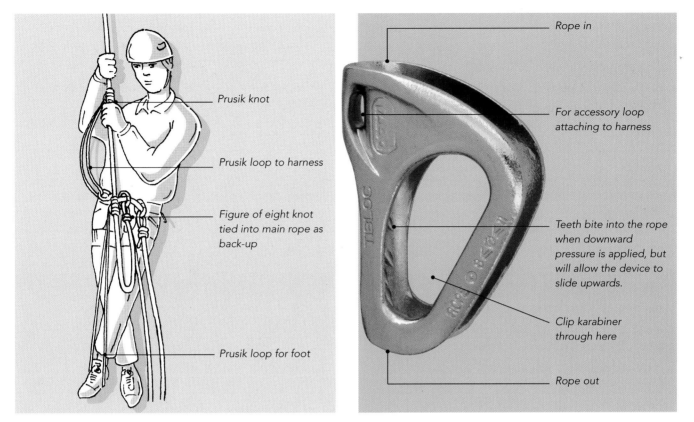

Prusik knot

Prusik loop to harness

Figure of eight knot tied into main rope as back-up

Prusik loop for foot

Rope in

For accessory loop attaching to harness

Teeth bite into the rope when downward pressure is applied, but will allow the device to slide upwards.

Clip karabiner through here

Rope out

Above left: If you are on a single rope, then tie a figure of eight knot in the main rope at knee level and attach it to your harness, untying and retying every few metres as a back-up.

Above right: The Tiblock is an alternative to using the prusik knot, for ascending a rope in emergencies.

TIPS ON PRUSIKING

- Prusiking can be quite strenuous for the uninitiated. Practise under calm conditions, rather than wait until you sit dangling in midair wondering how you are going to attach these fiddly little bits of cord to your rope, while the leader sits on an airy stance wondering if there is cellphone (mobile) reception.

- If you are climbing on double ropes, then prusik on one rope while the leader belays you on the other. If you are on a single rope, then tie a figure of eight knot in the main rope at knee level and attach it to your harness every few metres as you ascend the rope, untying the old knot every time you tie a fresh one, just so that you are not relying fully on one piece of prusik cord at any time.

- Prusiking is also useful if you are following a route, and find you can't manage a few moves on the very hard crux pitch on an otherwise reasonably graded route. No problem, simply whip out the loops, attach, jug up over the crux, and you're on your way.

- There are a few devices on the market that can be used in place of the prusik cord, e.g. a Tiblock (see above). These are small, light and work extremely well. The beauty with these is that you don't have to remember the prusik knot.

ADVANCED
PRUSIKING/JUMARING

Most climbers will only use prusik loops in an emergency, but prusik-ing is also used extensively when scaling big walls or steep snow slopes on Himalayan-style expeditions. In these cases it is more often referred to as 'jumaring' or 'jugging' and the basic prusik loops are replaced with ascenders, which clamp onto the rope.

Jumar clamps are specifically designed for the job. They lock onto the rope and slide freely upward, but lock when pulled in a downward direction. Most come as a left- and right-handed combination, with rubberized handles.

On a big wall, where climbers spend days, even weeks, trying to forge a route, fixed ropes are often used. This allows the climbers to abseil back down for a rest after a stint on the wall, or during a spell of bad weather. It also allows them to jumar up to their high point without reclimbing. This can involve hours of strenuous jugging up hundreds of metres of rope.

On big Himalayan expeditions, many of the steeper slopes and more treacherous areas are fixed with ropes, making repeated passage much safer. The climber simply snaps on the ascender clamp, then climbs/walks up the slope while sliding the clamp forward. Pulling on the handle assists your ascent and, in the event of a slip, the clamp will lock on the rope and prevent a fall.

Above: *A climber jumars up fixed ropes on the Old Man of Hoy, a 150m (500ft) sea stack on the Island of Hoy off the north coast of Scotland.*

OTHER USES FOR
THE PRUSIK LOOP

Prusik loops or ascender clamps are also invaluable for setting up a hoist system, and in emergency procedures like escaping from the system (see p179).

Right: *Jumar clamp.*

Rope to anchor

Release trigger

One-way clamp

Rubberized handle

Above: A climber top-roping a route. The belayer pays close attention to the climber, hands firmly on the brake end of the rope and without slack build-up in the system.

Above: A top anchor on a sports route with the rope also running through the last bolt.

Top-roping

Top-roping is perhaps the simplest form of climbing. For most climbers top-roping was their introduction to the sport. It is quick and convenient. It can normally be done quite close to the car and seldom higher than about 20–30m (66–100ft). It looks very safe and a lot of fun, but nevertheless relies on the basic skills of climbing: solid anchors, good belay techniques, rope handling and sound all-round safety management.

Most climbing accidents happen close to the ground and could have been avoided by proper and attentive practices.

ANCHORS

The quickest and often the safest way to get a good anchor at a sport crag, is to get an experienced climber to lead the route you would like to top-rope, clip the top anchors and also the last bolt before the anchors. If the route is overhanging, or takes a diagonal line, then some of, or all the other bolts should also be clipped to avoid swinging out, or 'penduluming' across the wall in the event of a fall.

At the anchors the rope should always be clipped through at least one locking gate karabiner.

At a traditional crag you have to set up your own anchors at the top, using traditional equipment.

A huge pine tree at the top of your route would be an excellent anchor, but this is rare good

TOP-ROPING TIPS

• Never use only one anchor point. At least one or two other anchors should be used as a back-up. In the case of a bolted route, both anchors must be clipped into. Also clip into the closest bolt below the anchors if possible. This eliminates the possibility of total anchor failure.
• Belaying is not something you run through quickly and then get on with the show. Climbers put their lives, totally and unequivocally, into the hands of the belayer, who should be confident and efficient. If not, then there should be an experienced climber monitoring the situation.
• Climbing is equipment-reliant, and harnesses and belay devices should be fitted properly to climber and belayer at all times.

Above: A cordelette is used here to equalize the force on all the points of the anchor. Screwgate karabiners can be used to bolster the security of the anchor.

fortune. Never skimp on an anchor. Use as many pieces of gear as necessary and spread the load. Avoid using the same crack for all four pieces of gear that constitute your anchor so that not all your pieces are rendered useless if the crack crumbles.

The load must be equalized across all the points of the anchor. In the event of a fall, no one piece should take the brunt. This can be done in several ways, depending how close the points are to each other. A cordelette is quick and efficient, but if the anchor points

Above: *The belayer is anchored to the ground to avoid being pulled forward or upward in the event of a fall.*

are spread out, some slings may be necessary to extend them.

Always make sure that the point where the rope runs through the top anchors hangs over the edge of the crag and that the rope hangs free and runs smoothly with the least friction or abrasion.

BELAYING

Make sure that the rope is threaded through your belay device properly and clipped to your harness belay loop with a locking karabiner.

The climber and belayer should always check each other's

equipment and harness. Does the belayer have the device clipped in correctly? Do the climber and belayer both have their harnesses on snugly and the straps doubled back through the buckle?

Before the climber sets off, the belayer should also make sure to be standing in the right position, in a straight line with the anchor and close in, to avoid being pulled off balance by a fall. If the climber is much heavier than the belayer, there should be an anchor point on the ground.

As the climber starts up the pitch, it is important that the belayer keeps the rope fairly tight for the first few metres, since a fall near the start of the pitch involves more rope, and therefore more rope stretch – and a potential 'deck fall'.

As the climber proceeds up the pitch the belayer takes in the rope through the belay device, ensuring that the brake hand is never released.

At the top of the pitch (at the anchors), the climber will shout down to the belayer: 'Take!' The belayer pulls in any slack in the rope and takes in as much of the rope stretch as possible and holds that position. The climber then sits back in the harness and calls down to the belayer: 'Lower!' The belayer then lowers the climber smoothly and steadily to the ground, often using both hands in the brake position.

TRADITIONAL (TRAD) AND BIG WALL CLIMBING

Roped climbing can roughly be split into two disciplines: traditional climbing and sport climbing. Sport climbing, where the climber uses pre-placed bolt protection, is relatively new. Traditional climbing (or trad climbing), on the other hand, goes back a long way and has evolved through the years mainly due to technological advances in equipment. It involves two or more climbers on a single- or multipitch route from the bottom up, placing all protection on lead, setting up stances, being self-sufficient and leaving little trace of their passage.

Above: Black Rocks, Cromford in the Derbyshire Peak District – a long and delicate stretch on Longships, which takes an uncompromising line up a vertical wall.

Leading

In most cases, one person will always take the lead. It does happen, of course, that two climbers of equal experience and ability will share the lead, accept equal responsibility and make democratic decisions on a climb, but generally the onus will fall on the shoulders of one person.

The leader on a multipitch climb not only leads each pitch, sets up safe stances and makes sure the following climbers are safe, but also takes on the role of overall leader. This means taking responsibility for everyone in your party for the whole day, from the minute you shut the car door until everybody has returned safely to their cars after the climb. On big mountain routes this can be a huge and onerous task.

To become a proficient leader you should be experienced and competent in the physical as well as the general aspect of climbing.

Physical aspects of leading

You should be able to lead every rock pitch from bottom to top in a confident, safe and controlled manner. You need to look at the overall aspect of the route and be sure that you are skilled enough to lead the grade of every pitch on the climb.

THE ART OF LEADING A ROCK PITCH

As exhilarating as top-roping a climb may be, the main event only really starts when you set off on the lead. Your senses are sharpened and your focus is absolute. There can be no calls for 'tight rope' (see p86), or asking the leader for advice on a difficult section. You are out in front. All decisions are yours. You hold and play the cards that could determine success, failure or disaster. It sounds daunting, but the rewards are great: the feeling that rushes through your body as you reach the stance after a particularly demanding pitch. That is your reward for having read the rock well and pieced together the crux sequence; having kept your head and paced yourself physically. It is one of those extreme pleasures that can only be experienced when the mind crosses the boundary to leave behind the superfluities and artificialities of everyday life.

Before you tie into the sharp end, you must be proficient in rope management and well schooled in placing protection and arranging belays. Most importantly, you must have survival sense: knowing when to retreat is an important aspect of leadership.

MENTAL ASPECT

The mental aspect of climbing is the most difficult. Nervous leaders are never in control. They climb jerkily and grip the rock too tightly, expending energy unnecessarily. The more pumped, or further from their gear they get, the more nervous they get and the greater their chances of falling. Knowing this, they get even more gripped and so the circle continues. Placing protection under these circumstances is difficult and, if done rashly, can endanger everybody. The commitment is total and there should be no doubts in your ability to complete what you set out to do.

Above: A climber leads up one of many stemming routes on Devil's Tower, Wyoming, USA. Most of these routes are difficult and sustained, demanding experience and a good head.

CONFIDENCE VERSUS HUBRIS

Years ago, as a leader of little experience, I led a climb that was then at the top end of my ability. It was a long, steep crack that ended in an overhanging face that led to a small, sloping stance.

Almost as soon as I started I felt out of my depth. The first crux was difficult to protect. I pulled untidily through the bulge and nervously continued trying to find a place where I could stop comfortably to place gear.

I climbed into the danger zone, where a fall would have meant hitting the deck from about 10m (33ft) up. My friends were calling to me to place gear, but I was too scared to stop: my arms were tired and I wanted to find a place where I could get a hands-off rest.

I found a little ledge where I could recover a little, place some gear and assess the rest of the pitch. I was now up to my ears and way past the point of no return. I continued jerkily upwards and got tired quickly. I couldn't stop to place gear, because I knew I wouldn't have enough strength to hang on with one arm while I placed anything. I continued, again hoping to find a place where I could get all the weight off my arms. It never came. I clipped an old piece of faded and frayed rope, which was attached to an old nut wedged deep in the crack, and remember thinking to myself: 'I hope I don't have to rely on that piece of old tat to hold a fall.'

I climbed on and soon my forearms were so pumped that I couldn't climb another move up. I looked down and saw that old piece of blue tat winking at me about 5m (16ft) below my feet. I had a bright idea. I would down-climb to the blue tat and rest there. An experienced climber would have known that if you haven't the strength to climb up, you won't have the strength to climb down. With my first move down, my hands simply opened involuntary and I felt the air whistling through my helmet. I came to a stop 10m (33ft) down. The blue tat had held. I had broken all the rules but came out with a warning.

Above: Climbing a low-angled slab relying on friction only for upward progress.

Above: A standard rack of gear, consisting of a set of quickdraws, a selection of cams covering most sizes and a good selection of wired nuts.

READING THE ROCK

Another function of the leader is to read the rock correctly when applying a route description to a climb on a rock wall. Start on easy, low-angled climbs where you can concentrate on the job and not worry about conserving strength, or hanging on by your fingernails while placing protection.

Choose a route that you have done a few times before, on the safe end of the rope and, preferably, go with an experienced leader, who can guide you in your journey to becoming a capable leader yourself.

RACKING YOUR GEAR

Before you even set foot on the rock you must have your gear racked in such a way that you know where everything is. When you spy a likely looking crack that will take a #5 wire, or a #0.75 camming unit, you must know exactly where to find it in your rack, so that time is not wasted searching for it.

The method of racking gear depends on the individual and you will soon develop your own system. Some rack their gear on their harness, while others prefer to use a bandolier (a sling over one shoulder).

It is often difficult to guess the exact size needed. You might try a #5 wire, to find that it is slightly too big and a #4 would fit better. For this reason it is better to rack similar sizes together on the same karabiner, so that you won't need to go back to your harness, since you will already have it in your hand. Just switch nuts and place the more suitable size. The other nuts are then reclipped to your harness loop.

THE WELL-SORTED RACK

Most harnesses have four gear loops, two on each side. Rack all your camming devices on the right front loop. Put your three smallest cams on one karabiner, arranging them in order of ascending size. The next three sizes on the next karabiner, and so on, but stop short of the really large cams unless you know for certain that the climb you are about to do definitely needs that over-sized piece. Carrying large camming devices can often be more irritating than they are worth, since they tend to get in the way and catch on edges.

Above: *The front gear loop, showing well-racked nuts and quickdraws.*

Above: *The gear loop on the other side, with well-racked cams and quickdraws.*

Above: *The back gear loops of the harness where other pieces of gear and necessary items can be clipped, like your belay device, spare karabiners and prusik loops.*

After sorting out your cams, arrange a selection of about 15 wire nuts onto two karabiners, sorted by size into two bunches of seven or eight each, and place these on the left front loop. Then rack about five quickdraws on each side behind the cams and wires, but still on the same loop.

The back loops on your harness are used for your belay device, nut remover, the odd piece of gear that you may want to add to your rack, spare karabiners or quickdraws, prusik loops, walk-off shoes, windbreaker and perhaps a small pouch containing an energy bar and juice.

To finish off your rack you will need about four or five slings, some 60cm (24 in) and others 120cm (48 in) long. These are slung around your neck and one arm, with one or two karabiners attached to each one. Some climbers also like using a selection of hexcentric nuts. The small to medium sizes can either be on wire or a short sling and can be attached to your harness on one of the back loops. Bigger ones are fixed to a 60cm (24 in) sling, which is then slung over the shoulder, but these are optional.

This is a good standard rack suitable for most routes, but you will modify your rack to suit the climb you are doing. For instance, if you are climbing a 60m (200ft),

almost uniform crack about 5cm (2 in) wide, then you can do away with the very small and overly large gear and rather double or treble up on your medium-sized pieces.

Above: *Climbing Belly Full of Bad Berries at Indian Creek, Utah, USA. On the almost uniform cracks in this area you need to double or treble up on certain sizes of equipment.*

Setting out

Before setting out on the sharp end, study the pitch you are about to climb. Break it up into climbable chunks separated by ledges, big foot holds, or places where you think you will get good gear placements. Stay calm and climb slowly and confidently, keeping your focus sharp and your senses alert and remember to breathe. Look ahead while climbing and figure out in which direction the pitch is likely to go. This way you will avoid climbing into a dead end, which can be hard to down-climb.

PLACING GEAR

When leading, your senses are sharpened. You are focused. Your eyes scan the rock continuously for sites to place gear, assessing every crack, pocket and orifice. When setting off on the lead, always try to place a 'bomb-proof' piece of gear as close to the stance (*see glossary*) as possible. This will remove the chance of a factor two fall (see p53) and avoid putting huge strain on the belay anchors, belayer and climber in the event of a fall. As you progress up the pitch, place gear regularly. Place back-ups for mediocre gear placements where possible and also before crux sections.

Beware though, that in your eagerness, you don't place too much gear and find yourself short with 10m (33ft) to go! Pace yourself, so that your gear will last the full length of any given pitch.

Above: *The climber on the right has used extensions on every piece of gear, thereby reducing the angle of the rope as it passes through and thus reducing rope drag. The climber on the left has failed to do so, which will result in major rope drag.*

Climbing a pitch smoothly and in control is an unsurpassed joy. However, there is one enemy that spoils the pleasure on the rock: rope drag. The rope must flow behind you in a more-or-less straight line. This is dictated by the line of your protection, so make sure when placing each piece of gear that the rope won't be forced to change direction sharply, thereby putting a kink in the rope. Mostly, this can be avoided by extending the sling on the gear to reduce the angle. Other causes of rope drag are going around corners and over roofs. Always extend your gear in those cases, so that the rope does not catch on the lip of the roof. Severe rope drag is unpleasant and can be debilitating (see Eliminating rope drag p116).

Stance set-up

Setting up a good belay stance is the basis of safe climbing. Anchors must be solid enough to hold a fall of any proportion and accept forces from several directions. At least one solid piece must be able to take a general downward pull. This must be backed up, depending on availability of gear (and cracks in which to place it). Then you should check where the forces will be coming from in the event of a fall. The pitch may start with a horizontal traverse out to the right. In this case the force will come from the right side and your stance must include at least one piece of gear that can withstand a pull in that direction. In many cases a solid nut or cam placement can accept forces from more than one direction and can be used as your standard downward pull as well as a directional piece. If the leader is climbing directly above the stance, which is often the case, then a bombproof anchor that can hold an upward pull must also be placed. A stance should have at least three solid pieces, preferably more, particularly if few really trustworthy placements can be found.

EQUALIZING THE ANCHORS

Once you have placed your gear, you need to attach yourself to the anchors in such a way that no one piece will take the brunt of the force in the event of a fall. This is called equalizing the anchor.

When tying into the various anchor points you can use slings, quickdraws, a cordelette, the rope, or a combination of some, or all of these. It depends on what will work best at a given stance and what you are used to working with. Whatever is used, the important factor is that all the anchor points must be weighted equally. Here the clove hitch comes into its own, since it is an easy knot to adjust while still tied into the karabiner.

Three solid anchor points

Cordelette tied to all the anchor points to equalize them

Climber tied to anchor from his belay loop

Belay device clipped to belay loop

Rope going down to climber

Left: At this stance the climber is well set up to an anchor equalized using a cordelette. Screwgate karabiners can be used to bolster the anchor. The climber is hanging in a comfortable position and is ready to belay.

HANGING STANCE

A hanging stance is more awkward to set up because there is no ledge to stand on while setting up your stance; you have to do it standing on small holds, while hanging on with one hand. It is also an uncomfortable stance from which to belay, since you'll be hanging in your harness, which can be a tad uncomfortable, depending on how long you have to hang around for.

Another concern is where to put all the coils of rope that you are pulling in while belaying. If the route is overhanging, it may be fine to let the rope hang straight down the face, but be very careful of this practice, since a gust of wind can blow a coil of rope around a stout bush, or into a crack, and jam it irretrievably. On less steep faces, or slabs, ropes have an uncanny ability to latch onto the smallest of knobs and wrap themselves around tiny flakes, making your life more colourful than necessary under the circumstances. Keeping your ropes tidy is an integral part of a good working belay stance, be it a hanging stance, or a big ledge.

Right: *A typical hanging stance where the climber has no ledge of any kind to stand on and must sit in his harness while belaying.*

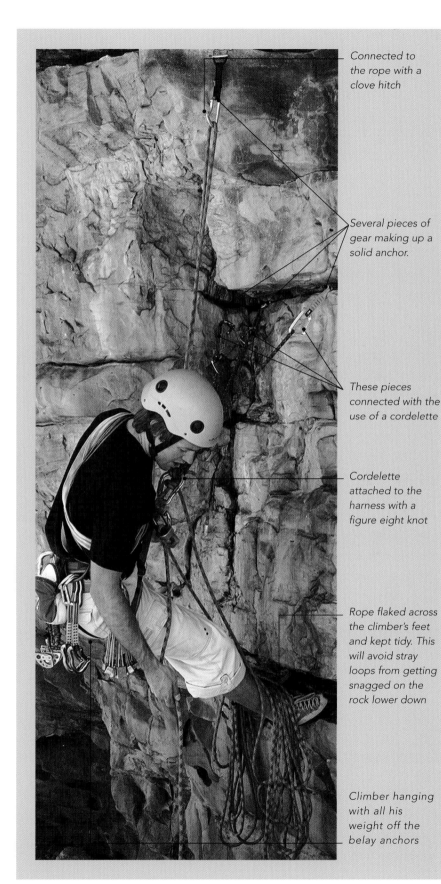

Connected to the rope with a clove hitch

Several pieces of gear making up a solid anchor.

These pieces connected with the use of a cordelette

Cordelette attached to the harness with a figure eight knot

Rope flaked across the climber's feet and kept tidy. This will avoid stray loops from getting snagged on the rock lower down

Climber hanging with all his weight off the belay anchors

KEEPING THE STANCE TIDY

On a hanging stance, the rope can be draped over a sling attached to one of the anchor points; across your lap; or over the top of your ankles to avoid it sliding into the void below. You need to keep it tidy so that when you have to feed from the pile on the next pitch, you will want the rope to come away without tangles. This is great in theory, but I have yet to meet a climber who hasn't had a birds-nest experience on a hanging stance. There is only one piece of gear that can work reasonably well in these situations. This is the Ringo. It has a bendy, but rigid hoop with an opening on the one side where the coils of rope are laid through. As you pull in the slack, just flick the rope through the coil every 5m (16ft) or so and your rope can be kept neat and tidy with the least amount of effort.

On a normal stance, where one is standing on a ledge of sorts, keep the ropes in a neat pile and not strewn all over the place. This ensures smooth running, especially when belaying the next pitch and the rope needs to run smoothly off the top of the pile. If the leader is leading with the rope from the bottom of the pile, turning the pile upside-down will assist matters.

Belaying with two ropes will compound the problem and more attention should then be given to rope management. If two 60m (197ft) ropes get amorous with each other, it can sometimes take a lot of time and patience to untangle the mess.

Open loop through which coils of rope are slotted

Above: *The Ringo is a lightweight split ring, especially useful on a hanging belay, which helps to coil the rope neatly.*

Above: *It is easy enough to keep your ropes neat when you're belaying from the ground, but when on a narrow ledge (as here), or on a hanging stance (see p113) more care is required.*

Double rope technique

Any form of traditional climbing can be undertaken with single or double ropes. Double ropes give much more flexibility in most situations and their use is advisable when climbing multipitch traditional routes.

In fact, it is good practice to always throw those double ropes in your pack when you are off to climb a trad route, since you never know when you will need them. It has many benefits and the only disadvantage is the weight of the rope, but then it is possible to split the weight between two people. With a single rope, the whole bundle has to be shouldered by a single person.

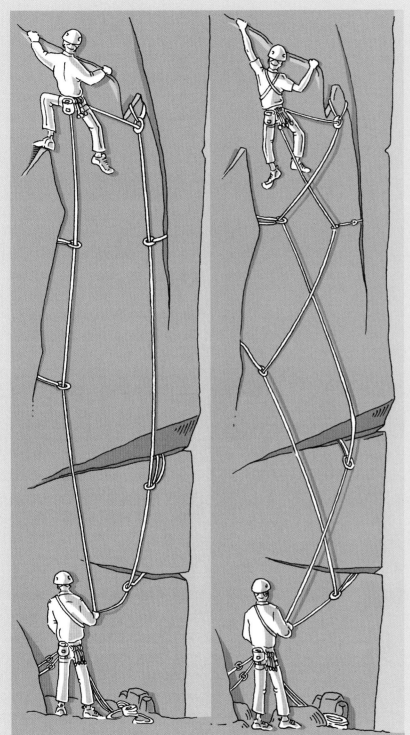

Above: *Whereas both climbers are using double ropes, only the climber on the left has alleviated rope drag by clipping them to run in a fairly straight line.*

Benefits of the double rope system

BACK-UP

It is comforting to know that if one of your ropes is damaged in a fall, you have another as back-up. This applies to leading as much as to following. I can think of many occasions when, following a difficult traverse with sparse protection, I thanked the Rope Gods for the two ropes snaking out into that void, rather than one thin strand.

It is more important when leading, since a fall is then almost always more severe. While leading, it is vital to keep a conscious check on how your ropes are running, not least because you want to avoid letting your ropes run over sharp edges, or through notches or cracks, which could damage the rope in the event of a fall. This is sometimes unavoidable and a back-up rope in these circumstances is reassuring.

On multipitch mountain routes, ropes lying on ledges are always in danger of being struck by falling rock. If one of your ropes is damaged by falling debris, you stand a much better chance of getting yourself out of a pickle if you have one full length rope to fall back on (excuse the pun).

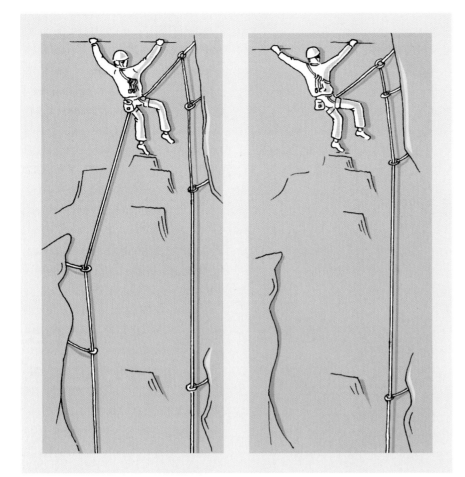

Above: *With only one rope, the leader has to compromise between rope drag or fewer protection points. With double ropes the leader can place more protection – and clip them in a straight line to reduce rope drag.*

FLEXIBILITY AND FREEDOM

When setting out to climb a trad route you have never climbed before, prepare yourself by getting a written route description and a topo diagram and by speaking to friends who have done the route before. Nevertheless, you have no way of knowing how the pitches are going to run. Not only are no two pitches in the world the same, but there is often more than one way to climb a pitch, depending on how the leader reads the rock and on individual style of climbing. The double-rope technique gives you the necessary flexibility and freedom of movement to cope with most eventualities.

ELIMINATING ROPE DRAG

One of the most debilitating factors a leader has to deal with, is rope drag. In fact, it is a leader's second-worst nightmare after a death fall on a crumbly runout. It weighs you down and frustrates the life out of you when trying to clip a runner. Pulling in the slack against rope drag when belaying your second, pumps you out worse than climbing a hard pitch.

For me one of the prime reasons for using double ropes on a trad pitch is to give myself as much freedom of movement as possible. By that I mean being able to move freely on any given pitch and not governed by rope drag. This is especially important when it comes to an on-sight ascent (see adjacent fact panel).

Take for instance a pitch that has twin cracks running up a wall about a metre (a yard) apart. It would make the pitch much more enjoyable (and possibly easier), if you could use both cracks. Using both cracks will also give you many more options for placing protection. With two ropes you can use both cracks to place gear, clipping one rope through the runners in one crack and clipping the other rope through the runners in the other crack. This way your ropes are kept running straight with little or no rope drag. With a single rope you could only use one crack or you will be unable to move after one or two zigzags between the cracks (see adjacent illustration).

REDUCING THE LENGTH OF A FALL

Another advantage of alternate clipping, whether you are weaving about or climbing straight up a single crack, is the fact that you are seldom pulling in slack from your last piece of gear, but rather from the piece before that, thereby reducing the potential length of a fall if you fell while trying to clip.

Scenario A: You are leading with a single rope and are 3m (10ft) above your last piece of gear. You stop to place another piece and pull up slack to clip that piece. As you pull in the slack, you increase the length of a potential fall.

Scenario B: You are climbing with double ropes and reach the same point as above. However, this time you are pulling the rope running through the gear below the last piece and therefore not affecting the length of a potential fall. If you fell at the worst possible time (the point where you have pulled up enough slack to clip, but before having done so), your fall will remain the same, as you are now falling on the rope which has no slack in it.

MORE EFFECTIVE LOADING OF BELAY ANCHORS

Belay anchors have to take forces from multiple directions (see p112). This can be done more effectively with double ropes, because you can split the duties between them. For instance, one rope can be secured to the anchors that are set for a downward pull, while the other rope can be secured to the ones set for another specific directional pull. When attaching the rope to your anchors, make sure that there is no slack between pieces and that the whole system is snugly connected.

When belaying with double ropes it is practical to treat both ropes as one. When paying out the rope to the leader or bringing up a second and piling the ropes next to you on a ledge, it is not necessary to keep the ropes in separate piles. Having both ropes piled down as one normally works perfectly well. The only exception will be when the leader is pulling up

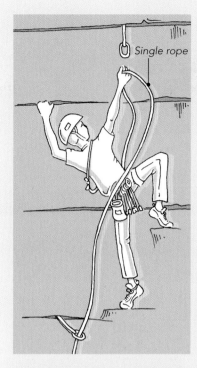

Single rope

Scenario A: *The climber pulls in slack to clip a runner. A fall at this point will be double the length of all the rope pulled up between the previous runner and the tie-in to the harness. (For the purposes of this illustration the rope is shown behind the body, although it is better for the rope to run in front of the climber's body.)*

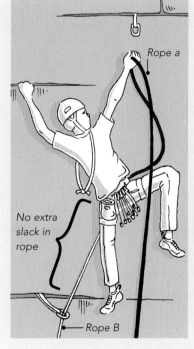

Rope a

No extra slack in rope

Rope B

Scenario B: *With two ropes, a fall at the same point will result in a much shorter fall, since the rope through the last runner, which will hold the fall, does not have any slack in it.*

one of the ropes to clip into a runner, then the second should only pay out the rope that is called for and keep the other rope as is.

PARTY OF THREE

Double ropes are also useful when climbing as a party of three. In this instance, the leader is tied onto both ropes as usual and the two followers are tied onto separate ropes. When the leader reaches the stance the anchor system is set up as usual. At this point the leader has a choice: bring the seconds up one at a time, or bring them both up at the same time. Belaying each one separately is probably safer, since each climber then gets undivided attention, but sometimes time is against you. On a long multipitch climb, for instance, the leader has no choice but to belay both at the same time. In this case, it is important that the followers are always a safe distance apart (about 5m; 16ft) so that the top climber will not land on the other in the event of a fall.

When climbing as a party of three it is also important for the leader to place protection with consideration for both climbers following. With normal alternate clipping of the ropes, you might inadvertently leave one of your followers facing a dangerous pendulum, since that might be the rope that you left out of a crucial clip on a traverse. A fair amount of experience is necessary for a leader to confidently and safely use double rope techniques under these conditions.

Above: *Belaying two climbers following simultaneously, the leader has to operate the two ropes separately.*

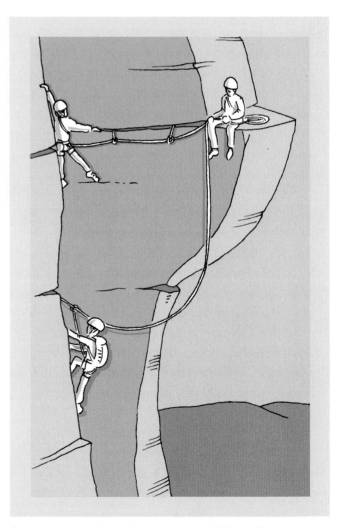

Above: *Due to bad gear placement second follower faces a pendulum once the last piece of protection is removed.*

LONGER ABSEILS (RAPPELS)

Many peaks and big mountain routes have no walk-offs: descent is by abseil only. In these situations double ropes (or twin ropes) are invaluable because, joined together, they will give you full rope-length abseils of 50–60m (164–197ft) rather than the 25–30m (82–98ft) abseils from a single rope doubled up. You will often find that abseil stations are spaced at 50m (164ft) intervals to accommodate double rope abseils only.

In the event of a retreat off a big wall, or even down a fair-sized multipitch climb, a two-rope system means fewer abseils and more choices when selecting your next abseil point.

EMERGENCY OPERATIONS

You are 100m (328ft) up a rock wall when your leader falls, hits a prong on the way down, breaking a leg, and comes to a stop under a large overhang. There is not enough rope to lower the injured climber back to your stance. The stricken climber can't prusik, or assist himself in any way because of the broken limb. You need to alert a rescue team, but there is no cellphone reception. The only way out is for you to 'escape from the system' and fetch help. However, you are 100m (328ft) up a rockface and your only rope is tied up on the pitch above, with the leader hanging off the other end. You only have 10m (33ft) of slack rope lying on the stance.

With double ropes, the picture would look a lot less hopeless: just get the leader to untie one of the ropes from his harness and pull the rope through to your stance. You now have one full rope with which to abseil off the route, while the leader is still hanging safely from the other rope. (See also Escaping from the system and other emergency procedures p179.)

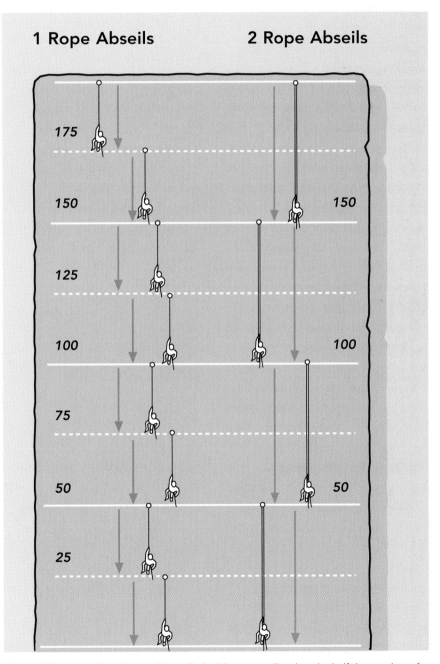

1 Rope Abseils　　**2 Rope Abseils**

Above: When abseiling down a big wall, double ropes will reduce by half the number of abseils you would have had to do with a single rope.

Protecting the second

When setting off up a pitch it is important to ensure that the gear protects not only the leader but also the second. This is particularly important when the pitch is diagonal, or has a traverse in it.

If the pitch goes straight up, then it is not a concern to get the protection gear working for the second. However, if there is a deviation in the line of the pitch, the second must be suitably protected, especially when a difficult section precedes an easy traverse.

For instance, the leader has climbed 10m (33ft) up a crack placing gear along the way. The crack now bulges and becomes difficult and strenuous for about three moves before a good handrail is reached. The leader, having checked out the pitch from the ground, has anticipated this, so now arranges some good gear at the start of the difficult section. This will ease the mind and set the leader up for the crux moves. After successfully completing the hard section, the leader thankfully latches onto the good handrail and rails easily across a low-angled wall for 5m (16ft) to a stance without placing any more gear, since the climbing after the crux is little more than trivial.

The leader sets up a belay and shouts down to you, the second, to follow. As you climb the crack, you remove all the gear that the leader has placed. You reach the bulging crux and, to your horror, realize that once you remove the gear so carefully placed to protect the leader through the difficult section, you will be totally unprotected and face a huge pendulum fall across the face if you botch the crux. This reduces the fun factor to minus 1000, particularly if there are protrusions (the force with which a climber hits a wall or a projection of rock after swinging across a face, is the same as hitting the ground after a fall of the same distance). This scenario could have been avoided if the leader simply placed a solid piece of gear in the rail after the crux section, before commencing the traverse.

When leading a traverse, place gear regularly and particularly after a difficult move. This can mean placing gear behind you, or slightly below you: awkward, but necessary – if you are to give your second an enjoyable day, instead of reason to throttle you gently when arriving wide-eyed at the stance after escaping impalement and probable death due to your nonchalant disregard for what happens behind you.

There will, of course, be places where it is not possible to place gear to protect the second. In this case the second needs to be an experienced climber and capable of handling such situations both physically and mentally. In a party of three, a back rope can be used for the middle climber.

In the top illustration the leader has not placed enough protection for the second to avoid serious injury in the event of a fall. The bottom illustration shows how the second should be protected on a traverse.

General aspects of party leadership

The general aspects of leading are every bit as important as being a proficient leader of a rock pitch. A leader is responsible for the well-being of the party while on the mountain, whether scaling a flaring overhanging crack, traversing a peak across unchartered terrain, or simply following a path over mountainous ground.

The leader is there to make decisions at crucial times and should have the experience and ability to carry out these decisions in a positive and assuring way. It is important that the leader is seen to be unwavering and confident in all actions, especially when under duress. This is the person in whom everybody has put their trust and, in some instances, to whom parents have entrusted their children.

GROUP MANAGEMENT

Apart from sound mountaineering skills a leader should also have good 'people skills' and the ability to communicate with the group in a manner that instills confidence and unity within the group.

At a crag a leader should ensure that everybody is secure and able to manage the allotted tasks so that they go home feeling satisfied with the day's accomplishments. The leader should assess the abilities of each member of the group and never take on a route that will overstretch anyone's abilities. This is not only dangerous for the per-

Above: Cenotaph Corner, Wales, in the United Kingdom. A leader should ensure the safety of everybody in the group and take note of belaying practices and general behaviour, requiring good management skills.

son in question, but can put the whole group at risk.

In emergencies (an injury or bad weather conditions) the leader should never show signs of distress, since this can cause others to panic. The leader must remain calm and always behave in a rational and reassuring way.

On a multi-pitch rock climb the leader arranges the order in which people climb according to their

Above: After climbing the serious and demanding North Face of the Eiger, tired climbers are then faced with the notorious descent down the complex West Flank, where some have died.

experience. For instance, the most experienced climber (besides the leader) should always climb last, so that the gear can be retrieved efficiently and advice can be given from below to an inexperienced climber when the leader is high above and out of sight.

The leader should keep the stance tidy and make sure everybody is securely tied into the anchors. This will avoid the 'bird's nest syndrome' with the ropes and facilitate fluent movement up the respective rock pitches. A good leader must ensure that everybody in the party is well equipped with the correct gear.

Descents

Never take a mountain descent for granted. It can turn out to be the most demanding part of your entire trip. The descent is always undertaken when you are tired and taxed after a long and sometimes complex climb. Your descent can involve anything from a cable car ride (if you are lucky), or a good path leading down to the meadows, or it can entail traversing over rough, unmarked mountain terrain, down steep gullies, even including a series of abseils.

Big mountains are unsympathetic to humans. There is no compromise. This is the time when you really have to keep your wits about you. It is premature to toast success on top of a peak, when the jaws of peril are waiting for that simple, but unforgivable, mistake.

PRE-ROUTE HOMEWORK

Pre-route homework can make the difference between an enjoyable day on the hill or leaving you some-what less enthusiastic about your next back-country experience.

ACCESS

Although not yet an issue in the UK or Europe, it is a good idea to find out beforehand if you need a permit to climb in the area of your chosen route or whether you will be crossing private land. You may need to phone a farmer or controlling body for permission, or buy a permit.

HOW TO GET THERE AND APPROACH WALK

Where to park your car and finding the start of the approach walk to the beginning of your climb can often be one of the 'crux pitches' of the day, especially if you have to drive through a farm on unmarked dirt roads. Get exact directions, preferably from someone who has already been there, or a good large-scale map of the area.

Once there, and having shut the car door behind you, you still need to get to the bottom of the climb. Some routes have quite complex approach walks and should be well checked out before you blunder onto the slopes in the pre-dawn light. Here again, your best source of information is someone who has done the walk-in.

ROUTE INFORMATION

When setting out to climb a long multipitch route, you should have an accurate route description of the climb. This can be a pitch-by-pitch written description, a topo diagram, a photograph with a dotted line showing the route, or a combination.

Ask around. Find someone who has climbed the route, recently if possible. All and any information is useful. What is the rock like? Are there sections that you need to watch out for? Where is the crux and what is it like? Is there anything special you need to know about the crux, like hidden holds, for instance? What gear is most useful? What are the stances like? Are there any hanging stances? How long did it take them? Ask if there is anything else worth knowing: an eagle's nest, for instance, that should be avoided.

All this information will enable you to know what to expect as the climb unfolds and also gauge whether you are making good time or not.

WEATHER

A reliable weather report is vital. Setting out on a long route high in the mountains is not advisable if there is any threat of inclement weather. However, keep in mind that, unless it is a special mountain forecast, a weather report is mainly geared towards what will be happening in the low-lying areas and in the towns and cities. You need to extrapolate that to the surrounding mountains. It is quite common to find yourself fighting your way through a blizzard, while people are in shirt sleeves in a valley only a few kilometres away.

DESCENT ROUTE

Find out as much about the descent as possible. Find out which route to take, what landmarks to look out for and how long it should take. Check if there is water to be had anywhere en route. You need to know if there are decent bivouac sites along the way, in case you are caught out in the dark or if the weather turns.

LAST MINUTE CHECKS

A few last checks the day before your big climb can be vital. Have you got all the correct climbing gear? Did you pack emergency clothing like a warm fleece and a good water-proof top? Check your rations. It is advisable to throw in a few extra energy bars, or similar, in case of a forced bivouac. Do you have enough water? Did you pack that all-important headlamp, with spare batteries? Do you have a small first-aid kit, a cell phone (mobile), route description and all other route information? Last, but not least, always tell someone where you intend to climb and when you expect to return.

Above: El Capitan dominates the entrance to Yosemite Valley. There are many routes up El Capitan, all of them huge, exposed and terrifying. The Nose is the best-known route. Most parties climb it in more than four days, but that means hauling a lot of food and water. The better strategy is fast and light. The Roof pitch is indicated with an arrow.

Big wall climbing

Big wall climbing has its roots in Yosemite Valley of the USA, way back in the 1950s and 60s. Indeed, the most famous and most frequently climbed big wall route in the world was opened on Yosemite's El Capitan in 1959 by the somewhat incorrigible Warren Harding. The route is, of course, The Nose. Since then big wall climbing has spread its tendrils across the world to some of the most inhospitable and far-flung territories imaginable: places like Baffin Island, the Himalaya, Patagonia and Antarctica.

WHAT IS BIG WALL CLIMBING?

Any steep, unbroken wall of 500m (1640ft) or more that demands lots of artificial (or aid) climbing (see p16), and requires two or more days of swinging in the vertical world, can be regarded as a big wall. However, it is rare that a big wall will not involve a few short sections of free climbing (see p15 ch1). Indeed, some of the benchmark big wall aid climbs of the 1950s and 60s have now gone entirely free (some climbed in less than a day), but they are still regarded as big wall routes.

WHAT EXPERIENCE IS NEEDED TO CLIMB A BIG WALL?

Before embarking on your first big wall climb, you would need to have a good grounding in general trad climbing and to have climbed some fairly long routes, so that you will have the feel for being on the move for the entire day. It is also imperative that you have some practice in artificial climbing. This will entail finding some short routes on which you can sharpen your aid claws.

As opposed to free climbing, where the climber relies solely on the hands and feet to scale the rock, artificial climbing involves the mentally demanding game of using standard and specially designed equipment placed, jammed and hammered into various slots, cracks and orifices to support the climber's weight while moving from piece to piece to gain height. These pieces of gear are sometimes placed so precariously that they can barely hold the climber's body weight. On difficult big wall routes it can happen that 20–30m (66–98ft) sections are climbed relying solely on gear that can hold no more than a climber's weight. By practising on short routes you will pick up valuable tips on how best to place gear, learn what is solid and discover just how far you can push the boat out on shaky gear. You will get to understand the rock and how to tell the difference between placements in good rock, as opposed to dubious rock. Believe me, you do not want to stand on the first mashie you have ever placed, 300m (1000ft) above terra firma, not knowing if it will hold or rip.

On practice climbs you will also figure out how best to arrange

Above: *The Great Roof pitch (indicated with a white arrow on the picture opposite) of The Nose route on the 1000m (3000ft) granite monolith, El Capitan. Aid ratings are based on the number of 'body weight' placements in a row. But the difficulty of a wall climb also depends on other factors like the weather and length of the climb.*

your rack of gear (which can be very substantial) and how to work with all the different types of aid gear that you will need to drag with you.

The art of aid climbing is the ability to string and rig a pitch of rock with gear that is solid enough for a climber to hang from and, preferably, also to hold a fall.

Theoretically, if you can climb a difficult 20m (66ft) aid pitch, then there should be no reason why you can not string 20 or 30 similar pitches together and scale a 1000m (3300ft) big wall. In practice it is less simple than that.

ADDITIONAL EXPERIENCE

Climbing a big wall is not only about swinging around on aid gear. It also involves living on a vertical wall for a few days (or weeks). This means taking extra gear that will allow you to survive for this length of time: loads of food and liquid, sleeping gear and portaledges, cooking gear, all-weather clothing and some personal stuff like reading material. All this can weigh hundreds of kilograms and has to accompany you and your partner up 1000m (3300ft) of steep, unbroken rock.

All your gear gets sorted and packed into a big haul sack (or two). This sack is commonly known as the pig, the porker, or any name that conjures up a vision of a fat, heavy, round-bellied lump of lard. The pig should be made of good, hard-wearing fabric, that can

Above: A portaledge bivouac on the Central Tower, East Face, of the Torres del Paine in Chilean Patagonia.

withstand being grated against rough rock and have a webbing system that encompasses the bag, with attachment points that can be fixed to the end of the haul rope.

After every pitch the pig is hoisted up to the next stance. This can often be harder work than climbing the pitch itself. Learning

how to rig an effective hoisting system before jumping onto your first big wall will make life easier.

PERSONAL HYGIENE AND TOILET PRACTICES

In most cases personal hygiene and cleanliness take a backseat on big walls. The effort involved in

Above: Home from home, with all the climbers' belongings tied to a few points on the rocks in the Yosemite valley.

Yosemite, climbers used to just hang out from a solid anchor point and let nature do its job and hope that there wasn't an unfortunate soul wandering around at the bottom of the wall. Nowadays, however, it is illegal to let loose from the walls of Yosemite – and many other walls within the boundaries of national parks throughout the world. Because of this, and a general sense of responsibility to the environment, the poop tube was invented. This is an airtight PVC tube into which bags of faeces can be stuffed and kept sealed. It is disposed of in the sewage system after the climb.

When you have decided that you are ready to try your first big wall, it will be worth your while enlisting an experienced 'wall rat' as your partner and do a route that is familiar to that climber.

Climbing a big wall involves a lot of hard work and needs a strong will to succeed. It demands a good head in often perilous situations; the character to endure many continuous days in the vertical plain with yawning exposure as your ever present neighbour – and nary a ledge to rest a foot.

As your experience grows you will tackle bigger walls and more difficult routes, which can take you to remote parts of the world. The reverse is also possible, of course: after one big wall route, you may find yourself auctioning all your big-wall gear to buy a foot spa and a good book.

changing clothes and washing, or even just brushing your teeth, is simply not worth it. Normally climbers just hang in there until they are back at the fleshpots of civilization. If both of you are equally smelly, then there is no problem. Besides, more clothes means more stuff to put into the pig – when it is important to keep the pork sack as light and as small as possible.

Going to the toilet, however, cannot be sidelined for a few days and has to be addressed on any big wall. In the old days, when only a few 'hard-core dudes' were to be found scuttling up the big walls of

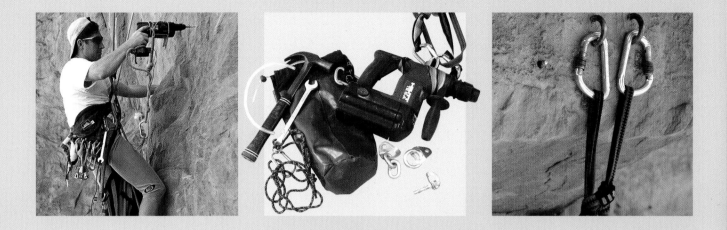

SPORT CLIMBING

The popularity of sport climbing is due to several factors. You do not require all the paraphernalia needed for traditional climbing (nor the expertise to use it), since the routes are all bolt-protected. This makes it much safer and more user-friendly. Generally, most sport crags have easy access, which eliminates long approach walks, thus enabling you to go climbing at almost any time of day. Packs will be relatively light, since equipment is kept to a minimum.

History

It all started when the French began to bolt difficult routes from the top down. Climbers then used to 'work' a particular route until they could successfully link the moves on lead. It took the rest of the world some time (and some convincing) to accept this form of climbing, but now there are hundreds of thousands of bolted routes scattered across every climbing nation on Earth.

Sport climbing equipment

You will need your own personal gear: a pair of climbing shoes, a harness, a chalk bag and a belay device with a locking karabiner. Between you and your partner you will also need a single 50–70m (164–230ft) dynamic rope (see p39), about 16 quickdraws and a few long slings.

What experience do you need for sport climbing?

If you go climbing with experienced climbers, you will need none at all, and you will pick up knowledge as you go along. However, if you are expected to hold your own in terms of belaying, leading and cleaning a route, then a fair amount of experience is mandatory.

Right: *The use of bolts forms an essential part of sport climbing, making it relatively safe and thus allowing climbers to push their personal limits.*

BELAYING

Being able to belay properly and safely is of paramount importance. You are fully responsible for arresting your partner in the event of a fall. But more than that, a good belayer is attentive and watches every move of the leader and pays out just enough rope so that the climber has neither too much nor too little slack.

LOWERING OFF

When a climber reaches the anchors, the belayer needs to lower the climber back to the ground. Good communication is needed here, to ensure smooth procedures. The climber at the anchors will shout 'Take me!' The belayer then takes in all the slack and as much of the rope stretch as possible, then shouts back, 'Got you!' The climber then releases the rock, sits back in the harness and calls to the belayer, 'Lower!' The belayer then lowers the climber back to the ground. Before climbing a route, both climbers should always ascertain that their rope is long enough to be able to lower off the route. A 30m (98ft) route needs a 60m (197ft) rope. If they are unsure, then a knot should be tied into the bottom end of the rope to prevent it from pulling through the belay device (one of the more common causes of accidents at sport crags).

CLIPPING QUICKDRAWS

There is nothing really difficult about clipping a quickdraw, but there is a wrong way and a right way to do it. A quickdraw (*see p41*) should have one karabiner for clipping into the hanger and another for clipping the rope. They should never be swapped, since falls on your quickdraw will leave rough scars on the inside curve of the hanger karabiner. A rope should never be clipped through this karabiner, because the rough edges can damage the sheath. Normally, the hanger karabiner has a straight gate and the rope karabiner has a curved gate, which allows the rope to be clipped more easily. When clipping the quickdraw into the hanger, always make sure that the back of the rope karabiner is (or will be) facing the direction in which you will be climbing. This will prevent the rope running over the gate. The most important thing about clipping the rope is that the rope must run from behind the karabiner and out through the front, to the climber. If clipped the other way, it is possible, in the event of a fall, for the rope to run backwards across the gate, thereby opening it quite easily and allowing your rope to become unclipped.

Avoid the 'second bolt syndrome': pulling up too much rope to clip the second bolt far above your head – you'll hit the deck if you fall. Rather climb to where you can clip without pulling up so much rope.

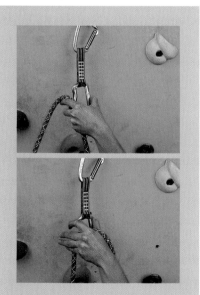

Top and above: *Clipping with the left hand when the gate is facing to the left.*

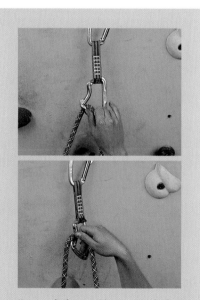

Top and above: *Clipping with the right hand when the gate is facing to the left.*

Cleaning a sport route

At the top of every sport route is an anchor from which you lower-off back to the ground and also where you will anchor yourself while preparing to clean the route. Whether leading or top-roping, a route has to be 'cleaned' after climbing. If it is you up there, be 100 per cent sure of the procedures, or you could end up a statistic. The anchor should comprise two bolts with either a hanger on each bolt and a chain attached to each hanger, or a length of chain tightened onto each bolt with a nut. You may also find two hangers with chains and a fat ring connecting the chain to one of the hangers. Whatever surprise you find at the anchors, the procedure is generally the same. (Never lower off a tape or rope anchor directly – the rope will burn through the anchor in a second with dire results.)

Clip two quickdraws (or slings) to your harness belay loop (NOT THE ROPE), then clip the other ends to the hangers at the anchor (if there are no hangers, then use the middle links of the chains). Pull up a metre or two of rope (3–6ft) and attach this to your harness or the anchor, using an overhand knot. This is to prevent losing your rope if you were to drop it after untying. Don't laugh: it can happen very easily – and if it does you won't think it funny. Untie the rope from your harness and thread the end through the last links of the chain, or through the fat metal ring, then re-tie the rope onto your harness. Undo the knot that you tied to prevent losing your rope. Check that everything is in order, and call down to your belayer: 'Take me!' Once you are certain that your belayer has you firmly on the rope, remove the two quickdraws from the anchor (and any other gear that may be clipped to the anchor), leaving only the rope threaded through the lower-offs. Now call to your belayer: 'Lower!'

On the way down, remove all the quickdraws on the route. If the route overhangs, then attach a quickdraw from the belay loop on your harness to the rope going through the quickdraws. This will keep you close to the rock and make cleaning the route easier. When cleaning after top-roping, then, for added safety, don't forget to back-clip the last bolt before the anchors on your way up.

Alternative method of cleaning a sports route:

1) Hang on the draws and take a loop of the lead rope.

2) Pull the rope loop through the anchors and clip the belay loop with figure eight knot and screw-gate karabiner.

3) Get the second to tighten the rope, then undo the tie in the knot.

4) Lower back down: tail just pulls through the anchor.

Different styles of climbing a sport route

Although this classification can also be applied to trad routes, they usually refer to sport climbing.

On-sight. The most coveted of all ascents. Without any previous knowledge of a route, the climber leads cleanly, first-off, without falls.

Flash. This is when a route is led first-off, cleanly and without falls, but the climber may have some previous knowledge of the route, or have watched someone climb it. Nevertheless, it is a first attempt.

Red Point. This is when a route is led cleanly and without falls after the route has been 'worked', or unsuccessfully attempted before.

Top Rope. The route is climbed with the rope coming from above.

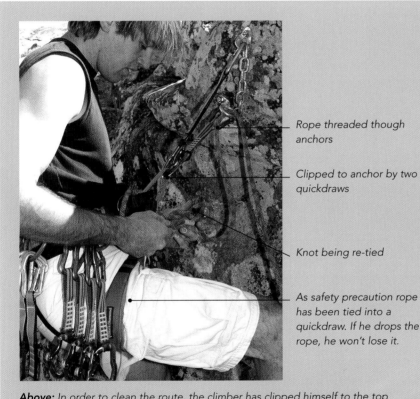

Rope threaded though anchors

Clipped to anchor by two quickdraws

Knot being re-tied

As safety precaution rope has been tied into a quickdraw. If he drops the rope, he won't lose it.

Above: *In order to clean the route, the climber has clipped himself to the top anchors with two quickdraws and untied the knot from his harness and threaded the rope through the chains. He is now tying back in to his harness, allowing him to lower off the route without leaving equipment behind.*

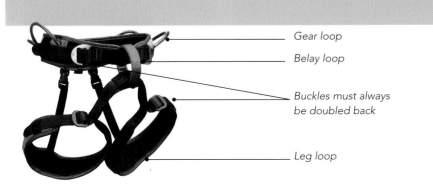

Gear loop

Belay loop

Buckles must always be doubled back

Leg loop

Bolting routes

Bolting a route is hard work, no matter how you look at it, and certain routes require more work than others, depending on the angle of the route and how difficult it is to gain access to the top anchors, for this is usually the point from which the bolting starts. However, there is always a certain amount of satisfaction after a hard day's bolting when you can stand back and admire your work.

FINDING A ROUTE

First one must find a decent looking line; preferably a line that jumps out at you, saying 'please climb me'. The route can be of any difficulty, but should be on good rock and aesthetically pleasing to the eye. Then make sure it hasn't been climbed before.

WHAT HARDWARE TO USE

Most sport routes today are bolted using 10mm (⅜ in) expansion-type, stainless steel bolts, or assorted stainless glue-ins. If bolting near the coast, then titanium glue-ins should be used. These are expensive, but will last longer than anything else in a salty environment. Expansion-type bolts need a hanger, which fits over the stud and is screwed into place, but once placed can be weighted immediately. Glue-in bolts need no hangers, but some types (U-shape) need two holes drilled and need a few hours for the epoxy to set before they can be

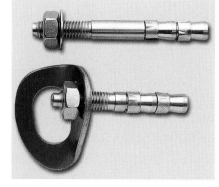

Above: Two different lengths of expansion bolt, with a hanger attached to the shorter one.

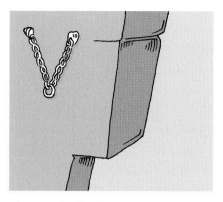

Above: Bolts should be placed at least 10cm (4 in) from edges and from other bolts at top belay or lowering stations.

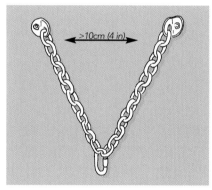

Above: One example of a lower-off anchor, with the correct distance between bolts.

Above: A typical glue-in U-bolt.

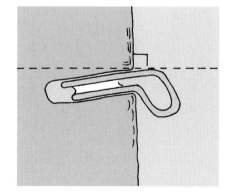

Above: The hole must be drilled at right angles to the rock. However, certain glue-in bolts should be drilled at a slight downward angle.

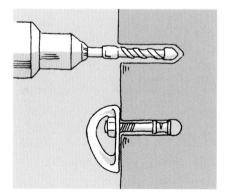

Above: A piece of tape around the drill bit helps to ensure drilling to the correct, pre-determined depth.

weighted. The advantage of a glue-in is that a climber can lower off any bolt on the route, because they are rounded. Hangers have a definite edge that will damage your rope.

Whichever bolts you decide to use, it is always a good idea to practise drilling a few holes and placing some bolts before you take to the hills. There is a certain amount of skill involved, and hanging on the end of a rope, with 15kg (33lb) of hardware and a drill throttling you, is not the best time to learn how to drill and place your first bolt ever.

BOLTING EQUIPMENT

A drill with a fully charged battery (or two, if you are in for a marathon session), rigged with slings and karabiners to attach to your harness or sling around your shoulders.

Drill bits. Different sized drill bits can be used, depending on whether you are using expansion bolts or glue-ins. Whichever ones you are using, be sure to take ample spares, since a drill bit's life varies a great deal, depending on the type of rock you are drilling into. Some hard rock like quartzitic sandstone allows only six or seven holes before your bit needs changing, while drilling into granite will get you 20 or more holes.

Blow pipe. This is essential for blowing the drill dust out of the hole and off the surrounding rock. This ensures better grip between the bolt sleeve and the rock.

BOLTING ETHICS

In some form or other, routes have been bolted for many years, but the practice is not universally accepted. In France, Spain, Italy and Thailand bolting is widely accepted, but in the UK traditional climbing still has a strong ethical foundation and bolting is frowned upon by many. Nevertheless, there are some dedicated sport climbing areas, Portland being the most prominent example, scattered throughout Britain. Ironically, you will find many an anti-bolting climber happily clipping bolts in the South of Spain or France. Back in Britain he might pen a vicious attack against some individual who placed a lone bolt on a mossy slab in an old disused quarry.

Hammer. This is needed for hammering the bolt into the hole.

Spanner. A size 17 spanner is used on 10mm (⅜ in) bolts for tightening the nuts.

Epoxy and epoxy gun. Make sure, when placing glue-ins, that you have the correct epoxy and an epoxy gun (dispenser). Bolt manufacturers can advise on this, but it depends on the kind of rock you will be drilling into.

A hold-all pouch. A strong bag for bolts, hangers and other hardware that you can hang off your harness for easy access while bolting.

Right: A climber with typical bolting gear. The drill is rigged with slings and karabiners for attaching to the climber's harness.

PLACING TOP-ANCHORS

You have found yourself an awesome line and are itching to bolt it and climb it. You have also decided that you are going to use expansion bolts and you have practised placing some in your mother's rock garden.

Your next step is to find a way to the top of the crag and to place a proper set of top-anchors. Sometimes this can be a simple case of walking around the side and up to the top, or in other cases it can involve trad-climbing up some horrible grotty chimney, or scrambling up chossy rock (see glossary).

Once on top, set up a trad anchor, so that you can abseil (rappel) down to the spot where you want to place your top-anchors. Once your anchors are set, you can set up a top rope through the bolted top-anchors.

MARKING THE ROUTE

Find the best places to put the bolts by top-roping the route and marking the spots where you want to drill. Particular care should be taken in the first 5–6m (16–20ft), since this is where a thoughtlessly spaced bolt can be the reason for a deck fall. Generally, near the ground, the bolts should not be far apart, but this can depend on the route. Top-roping a route can also give the climber a chance to work some of the moves and to clean any dangerously loose rock or bush off the climb, making it ready for the red point (see p131).

Bolts for a top anchor are offset, so that if one bolt were to fail, the other would still be in good rock

Large ring for threading the rope

Above: *A typical top anchor showing two bolts connected by a chain.*

BOLTING

Bolting can be done by jumaring up the route, or (which is more common) abseiling down. First you need to fully charge your battery, so that you don't run out of power with two holes still to drill, and check that you have enough bolts and hangers for the route which you are about to drill. Also check that you have all the other hardware that is necessary for the job. Lock your drill bit in the chuck and set your depth stick on your drill before you kick off on your abseil. Also check that your drill and hardware pouch are in a good position.

Abseil down to your first marker, make sure that the trigger lock is in the position that rotates the bit in a clockwise motion. The opposite way will have you drilling for hours with no luck. Keeping the drill as perpendicular to the rock as possible, apply pressure to the back of the hand piece, but not so much as to stifle the hammer action. This hammer action is very important and is what makes the drill-bit bite into the rock. Once you have drilled the hole to the correct depth, lock the trigger and let the drill hang by your side. Take the blow pipe and blow out the hole. Close your eyes while doing this and be careful that you do not inhale a lungfull of rockdust. Then, place a bolt in the mouth of the hole and gently tap the bolt until it seats properly.

Step 1: *When drilling the hole, ensure that the bit is perpendicular to the rock.*

Step 2: *Use a small plastic tube to blow dust out of the hole and off the surrounding rock.*

Step 3: *Hammer the bolt into the hole until only 1cm (½ in) is left sticking out.*

Step 4: *Tighten the hanger onto the bolt. Ensure that the eye of the hanger is directly below the bolt for optimal load bearing.*

Now hammer the bolt in until only a centimetre (½ in) is left sticking out. Put the hangers on the bolts before starting the day's bolting. Then you can hammer the bolts in with hangers already attached and avoid damaging the thread of the bolt between the nut and the hanger. Now tighten the nut on the bolt. As you tighten the nut, it will pull the bolt outward, forcing the sleeves to jam over the flanges, thereby wedging the bolt irretrievably. Be careful not to over-tighten the nut, since this may cause stress fractures.

If you are using glue-ins, then drill the holes required for the type of glue-ins you are using and blow out the holes. Apply epoxy into the holes almost to the top, using the epoxy gun, then push the bolt into the hole. Wipe off the overflow of epoxy and move on to the next hole. Be careful not to weight the bolt at all.

Repeat this procedure for every bolt, until you reach the ground. Your route is now ready for the red point (*see glossary*). For me, one of the best parts of bolting and opening new routes is that you get to name them. This is great fun and often leads to the most ludicrous names being bandied about, like Weasels Rip My Flesh, Pink Bubbles Go Ape, Catfish Rising, Red Guitar On Fire, Pink Harmonica In Ashes, A Man From Cockroach Land, Brahm's Third Racket.

BOULDERING AND SOLO CLIMBING

Once practised only to hone skills for climbing routes, bouldering has become a subculture of climbing, and is now a sport in its own right. Practised by millions of climbers the world over, it is the fastest-growing branch of the sport in climbing history. There are many brilliant, strong and talented boulderers out there, but the name that remains synonymous with bouldering is John Gill. Some of the feats of this American, who took bouldering to unheard of levels back in the 1960s, have still not been repeated, some for the sheer difficulty and others for the bold approach needed to climb them.

What is bouldering?

Climbing any piece of rock that is not high enough to warrant a rope can be called bouldering, but of course it is more complex than that. Bouldering is the art of linking a series of moves to complete what is termed a 'boulder problem'. The concept is to try problems that will push you to the limit of your physical strength and endurance; find the right sequence; and work at the problem until you 'send it'. This can take anything from an hour to a whole day, sometimes even weeks and, in some cases, years of trying, depending on the severity of the problem (and the ability of the climber).

WHAT DO YOU NEED FOR BOULDERING?

Bouldering is climbing in its purest form. Almost all equipment, like ropes, harnesses and protection gear, is dispensed with. All you need is a pair of climbing shoes, a chalk bag, a toothbrush for brushing off caked-up holds, some finger tape to reinforce your finger tendons for those seriously crimpy (see glossary) problems and a crash pad (padded mat). This is a 10cm (4 in) thick condensed foam mat covered in cordura material for good protection. It folds double and has shoulder straps to facilitate carrying to the bouldering areas. These mats are placed on the ground at the foot of a problem to cushion falls. A piece of old carpet or towel is also handy to stand on before launching onto a problem. This will keep grit and sand off the soles of your shoes.

Above: A boulderer tops out on a boulder problem. If the climber falls the spotters will control the fall and guide the falling climber onto the crash pad between them.

SPOTTING

Spotting is the bouldering equivalent of belaying. You stand very close to the boulderer with arms outstretched and ready to steady the climber in the event of a fall. This does not mean that you will catch the falling climber, but merely guide the fall in the direction of the mat and attempt to stop the climber from bouncing or falling over once landed.

For every boulderer there should be at least one spotter and, if the landing looks awkward, more than one spotter may be necessary.

THE ATTRACTION OF BOULDERING

Bouldering is not equipment intensive and can be enjoyed without the hassles of ropes and such like. It will also appeal to people who do not like exposure and would prefer not to get too high off the ground.

Being generally easily accessible and in pleasant surroundings, bouldering is normally done with a group of friends and can be quite a social event, with climbers egging each other on with words of encouragement.

BOULDERING TODAY

A few decades ago you could count the good boulderers on one hand. Nowadays, super hard problems are springing up all the time. Every time you open a climbing magazine there are more 8C problems and some that are

Above: *Topping out on slopers (see p69) is not an ideal ending to a problem. Here the spectators are watching rather than spotting.*

even given a provisional 8C+ grading. You will not find a route of, say, 20m (66ft) long, that involves moves as hard as the hardest boulder problem. The only reason that these super hard moves can be pulled off when bouldering, is because they are close to the ground, and you do not sap half your strength with 15m (50ft) of climbing before you reach the crux sequence.

This is also the attraction for top sport climbers, because they can concentrate on linking a series of incredibly hard moves, that would otherwise be impossible halfway up a 20m (66ft) face.

HIGH-BALL BOULDERING

In any form of climbing, there are always a select few who push the boat out a little further than the rest. In bouldering it is no different. Normally boulder problems take place on boulders that don't leave you dangling way off the deck. It is rare to get more than 2–3m (7–10ft) from the ground on any problem. But some climbers are not happy with nice, safe problems. They have to up the stakes and push into another dimension.

High-ball bouldering is where climbers boulder a little higher off the ground than most boulderers

Above: Bouldering in Chamonix, France, offers a beautiful setting, with Mont Blanc as a backdrop and shady forests.

would feel comfortable with. Some of these problems go over the 5m (16ft) mark and a few even approach 8–10m (26–33ft) above the ground.

To me this is more like soloing, although these problems still come under the banner of bouldering. During an attempt on a high-ball problem it is not unusual to have mats spread out over the ground, several deep, in addition to a bevy of spotters standing around with outstretched arms, waiting for the long plummet.

ENVIRONMENTAL ISSUES

Each form of climbing has its own set of environmental issues and bouldering is no different. When a particular boulder, or series of boulders, in an area is popular, it means that many climbers visit the area to climb on them. This can have a severe impact on the surrounding vegetation. Many mats are placed on the ground, often crushing shrubs and delicate plants underneath. Climbers can spend an entire day stomping around a single boulder trying various problems.

If you were to take before-and-after pictures of a bouldering area that has been frequented for about a year, you will be amazed at the difference in the vegetation around the boulders and between them, where climbers have walked from one boulder to the other.

Above: A solo climber makes a strenuous layback move on a crack at Burbage Rocks in the Derbyshire Peak District, UK.

Above: A climber soloing an exposed route on the sandstone walls of Table Mountain, South Africa.

Solo climbing

There are two practices that come under this heading: rope soloing is when a solo climber uses rope to self-belay; and free soloing is done without a rope. What drives a person to walk the thin edge between life and death? To risk all for a brief, momentary victory? When you climb high up on a rock wall without rope, the smallest mistake has the biggest consequences. It is unforgiving: the slightest miscalculation is unlikely to go unpunished. Solo climbers are generally regarded with bewilderment: are they insane? Do they have a death wish? To understand the attraction, you need only compare the difference in your focus and concentration when following a rock climb (the rope is above you), with when you are leading (the rope is below you and you are responsible for your own safety). Everything seems clearer and more crisp. Your mind is sharper, quicker, more calculating. Your eyes dart around, taking in all and retaining only what is necessary. Remove that rope and your focus takes a quantum leap into another dimension. Movements are clean, swift and deliberate. The mind blocks out all outside influences.

The solo climber is not a lunatic playing Russian Roulette, but an athlete at the very cutting edge of the sport: an athlete who, with superior mind control, pushes the limits of physical and (particularly) mental endurance.

Soloing demands serious mental discipline. There is no room for second thoughts or a change of heart.

Above: Jerry Moffatt, soloing an E1 5b gritstone route on Curbar Edge in the Derbyshire Peak District, UK.

Perched on a bulging rock wall 200m (660ft) above the talus slopes, feet on tiny smears and the finger tips of one hand supporting your body weight, commitment must be total. Any form of doubt is firmly locked out.

How does the soloist know what's ahead? What if he can't negotiate a certain section? What happens if he gets tired and can't hold on anymore? The answer to all those questions is that the soloist does not just pick a climb out of a hat. It is almost always a route that is known to the climber, sometimes intimately, and has great personal appeal. It is a carefully calculated game that does not allow for errors.

After a particularly fine solo climb, when everything has gone perfectly, the climber feels an elation that is incomparable. No drug on earth comes close.

Of course climbers get killed soloing, but then so do solo yachtsmen competing in extreme racing events, racing drivers, and a number of other sportsmen who live on the edge. However, statistically, few climbers are killed while soloing. Far more meet their end in the high mountains of the Himalayas and other, similar, ranges.

We are all more or less the same in body, but it's the spirit that makes the difference. Ernest Hemingway wrote. '*It takes more cojones to be a sportsman when death is a closer party to the game.*'

INDOOR CLIMBING
AND COMPETITIONS

Climbing gyms are made up of a series of wooden or resin-based walls of various shapes, angles and sizes. They are designed to resemble, to some degree, the rock faces of an outdoor crag. On these walls are bolted hundreds of artificial hand and foot holds of many shapes and sizes, made of a resin mixture, resembling real holds on a rock face. Some of the walls are designated for top roping only, with ropes hanging down from anchors, allowing climbers to try any of the routes. Other areas will have dedicated 'lead walls', where there will be bolts with quickdraws attached for clipping the lead rope. Most gyms also have a bouldering section.

Above: A typical indoor climbing gym, with a section for lead climbing, a top-rope wall on the right and a bouldering section with a continuous section of crash pads. There is also a seating area where climbers can rest and relax.

Why climb in a gym?

Climbing gyms have many uses: from staff team-building sessions in the corporate market, to kiddies' birthday parties. Children have a lot of energy and most of them love to climb, whether up trees or walls. Having a party at a climbing gym will keep them busy and happy for hours on end and deliver them back home exhausted at the end of the day. While these are probably a climbing gym's main sources of income, they are essentially by-products of the original purpose of the gym, which was to enable climbers to train between bouts of climbing on rock; to learn how to climb in the first place; and to hone their indoor climbing skills for competitions.

There are climbers who never venture outside the realms of the climbing gym: indoor 'princes of plastic' who have never felt the rough texture of genuine rock beneath their fingertips. This is of course their choice, but I would miss the reality of rock climbing and the ambience of a proper mountain crag.

LEARNING HOW TO CLIMB IN A GYM

Gyms are a great place to learn how to climb. The atmosphere is generally friendly. There are routes of all grades and angles and if you haven't come with an experienced climber who is willing to show you the ropes, then you can sign up for one of the gym's training courses. Most gyms offer a range of courses, from introductory to lead courses and some also do specialized courses concentrating on techniques and style, etc. A gym also gives the beginner a feeling of safety, so the anxiety felt when setting off up a rock wall is somewhat lessened. Once the budding climbers have learnt the basics, they will feel a lot more confident when they eventually set foot on their first real climb on rock.

Training

For most climbers the gym is a place to train, to get strong and improve technique and endurance. Some go for social reasons, to see old friends, meet new ones, spur each other on pumpy routes, and in the end getting a great workout. It is an ideal place for people needing a good physical challenge and who can accept total defeat and relish the excitement of getting a hard route.

Serious climbers use the gym for intensive training. They either work power or endurance at any one session. Often you will find a climber working a particular series of moves in a gym that simulate a series of moves on a rock climb that they are working. This will help the climber build the necessary strength for the moves and also to remember the sequence.

Warming up

Climbing gyms are designed to work the body intensively. Injuries develop easily and climbers nursing injuries should keep away. Routes in a gym differ from those at an outdoor crag in that a route in a gym is sustained at a particular grade, whereas on rock, normally, the opposite applies. For this reason it is important to warm up properly before any gym session. This can involve some stretches (I find 15 minutes of light

Top: *The gym is a good place to practise climbing techniques before trying them out at the crag. This climber is using a toe hook for balance.*

Above left and right: *A heel hook can help with balance and take weight off the climber's hands. The climber on the right is using an undercling hold to make upward progress.*

yoga does the trick), then jump onto some really easy climbs with big holds; maybe some slabby routes first, then progress to steeper stuff. Avoid the flash pump. If you feel the pump setting in, then step off the wall. Only start your preferred training routine once you are properly warmed up.

GYM TRAINING

Many climbers use the gym as they would a proper crag: they arrive with no particular plan in mind and just set about warming up. They gradually work their way up through the grades, giving themselves some hard challenges, and end off with some easier, but steep, routes to give them that final pump. Using the gym regularly (two or three times a week) for about six weeks will dramatically increase your strength and endurance. The next step is to concentrate on specific exercises and training to work key muscles and also to improve technique (see Training chapter).

GYM SAFETY

Gyms have safety regulations regarding the use of their equipment. They will also explain any rules to you when you join. They may prefer all climbers to use certain types of belay devices. Some general rules will apply wherever you go.

- Belayers must concentrate on what the climber is doing, despite distractions. You meet friends at a gym but, while chatting, your concentration is divided and a fall can catch you by surprise.

- When belaying or just walking across the floor, always be aware of what's happening above you. Most gyms have routes going up overhanging walls that stretch over towards the centre of the gym floor. A climber falling from the roof can come very close to the ground and possibly land on top of an unsuspecting belayer.

Top: *The climber is using the drop-knee technique to enable her to reach the hold with her right hand.*

Above: *The routes at a climbing gym are colour-coded so that a climber can choose the degree of difficulty or to practise specific techniques and holds.*

Competition climbing

It is human nature to compete. Even long before proper, sponsored and regulated climbing competitions began, there was rivalry among climbers. One of the more famous races was that for the first ascent of the Matterhorn in Switzerland between Briton Edward Whymper and the Italian mountain guide Jean Antoine Carrel. The first attempt was made in 1857 and the summit finally conquered on 14 July 1865.

The competitive element is always present in climbing circles, with much friendly rivalry between climbers at the local crags. It spurs people on to try

Above: *A climber takes an opportunity to shake out and chalk up while looking ahead and working out the next sequence of moves. Note that the climber is keeping the holding arm straight, so as not to put unnecessary strain on the muscles.*

harder and often gets you to push through a 'cruxy' section where ordinarily you would have given up.

The first climbing competition with proper rules and regulations was held in the early 1980s in the town of Arco in northern Italy. It was unique, in that it was held on an actual rock wall. Route-setters chipped holds into the blank rock to manufacture routes of escalating grades. It was a knock-out competition with the top climbers in each round going through to the next round, eventually culminating in a semifinal and final. Not surprisingly, the competition ended in controversy; the officials and judges themselves were still learning from the experience.

Climbing competitions have come a long way since then and today most competitions are held indoors on walls that are designed specifically for the job. They have been developed over many years and are masterfully crafted. It is a big business and a proper world-class competition wall can cost a tidy bundle.

Categories of competition climbing

DIFFICULTY COMPETITIONS

This this is the format of competitions in the World Cup circuit. Climbers compete on routes that increase in difficulty and only a handful of competitors from each round are selected to proceed to the next level. Routes for each round are set by official route setters and are changed before each new round.

Competitors are not allowed to watch other climbers climb the route, since this would give them an unfair advantage. Competitors wait in an isolation chamber and are only allowed into the arena when it is their turn to climb. They can, however, stay to watch those who climb after them.

Each competitor has to lead the routes and will climb until they fall or reach the anchors at the top of the route. If they fall before they reach the end, then they are lowered to the ground, their turn over.

The climbers who reached the highest point in any particular round, proceed to the next round and so on until the final round. A super final is held if two climbers tie in the final.

SPEED COMPETITIONS

Most speed competitions are also held on artificial walls, where two identical walls, with identical routes set on each, stand side by side. Competitors race each other up the routes using top-ropes through an anchor which is situated a few metres below a buzzer.

The first climber to hit the buzzer wins that round, then, much to the excitement of the crowds, the climber jumps off and takes a spectacular whipper of 5–6m (16–20ft) before the fall is arrested.

Recently, another form of speed climbing competition has evolved. Teams consisting of two climbers race each other up existing multipitch sport climbs. A typical example would be a six-pitch bolted route up a 200m (660ft) wall at a reasonably hard grade.

BOULDERING COMPETITIONS

Bouldering competitions have become increasingly popular over the last decade or so. Compared to 'difficulty competitions' they are simple to organize and cost a fraction because they avoid the logistical problems of huge, costly indoor walls; finding a suitable venue; and organizing a team of route-setters, judges and officials.

While some bouldering competitions are held on artificial walls, most are held outdoors on natural boulders in existing or sometimes newly discovered bouldering areas. A team of route setters will set a number problems of all grades on a large number of boulders. These problems range from quite easy to practically impossible – except for the demigods of bouldering.

Each problem is allocated a number of points (depending on the grade) and competitors are judged on each problem according to the style of ascent: whether on-sight, second or third try, etc.

At the end of the day, or within a certain time frame, all points are added up to give a result. If there is a tie, then the competitors in question will fight it out in a final round of problems. Most bouldering competitions are organized along these lines, but rules can vary from one competition to another.

ICE COMPETITIONS

These competitions are held along the same lines as the difficulty competitions, except that instead of having an artificial rock climbing wall, the competitors climb on an artificial iced-up waterfall. Water is run over a built structure and then frozen into a hanging waterfall. Routes are marked within borders of red lines and competitors must stay inside the marked lines. Kicking your crampons, or striking your ice axe outside these markers will automatically disqualify you. Climbers who climb the highest before falling will progress to the next round, until a select few reach the final.

Above: *A climber starts up on the lead during one of the rounds of a competition. These walls are continuously steep, so the competitors have to read the route carefully in order to climb efficiently and take note of potential rest spots.*

MIXED ALPINE AND HIMALAYAN CLIMBING

By definition, alpine climbing takes place in the high mountains. A route of alpine proportions will always have a certain amount of seriousness about it, whether it is the length, the difficulty, the conditions, the remoteness, or a combination of some or all of these factors. It doesn't necessarily have to include snow or ice climbing, but generally most alpine routes cover mixed ground of varying steepness.

To make the transition from mountain walker to alpinist is not as difficult as one would imagine. As an accomplished hill walker, you should have the necessary experience to deal with navigation in good and bad weather, to be able to see the signs of changing weather, and to be able to plan and carry out a long mountain trip.

You will, however, need to learn some techniques before embarking on your first alpine trip, such as the use of crampons and an ice axe, self-arrest and safe glacier travel, including crevasse rescue.

You will also need to acquire the knowledge and experience to read the mountains in terms of snow conditions: What is the condition of the snow? Soft, hard, rotten? Are the slopes prone to avalanche? If so, where is the best place to cross the slopes?

The best advice for any budding alpinist is to attend a beginner's alpine course. You will learn the basics of everything discussed in this chapter from experienced instructors and you will be given the opportunity to put it into practice. You will probably also do an introductory alpine route that will involve mixed ground, snow and ice. After that it is practise, practise, practise. Like any game, the more you do it the more honed your skills will become.

If you want to combine basic alpinism with classic alpine rock routes, then you must be proficient in rock climbing as well.

CRAMPONS

Climbing up or across steep ice or hard snow without crampons is close to impossible. Crampons come in two basic designs: flexible and rigid. The flexible type is fine for general mountaineering where you will mostly crampon flat footed on low-angle ice. They will also work for front-pointing, but then have to be matched to a rigid boot. If you are going to be climbing steep ice then it would be better to use rigid crampons. Crampons have 8–10 points facing down and two points facing straight out for front-

Above: A climber makes his way over mixed ground on a typical alpine route.

pointing. The first time you put on a pair of crampons, you feel a little clumsy and tend to stab yourself in the calf when trying to walk. They also ensure a head-first fall. Unless on easy-angled ground, a helmet is vital in winter climbing.

BOOTS

Plastic double boots will be many climbers' first option, since they are totally waterproof and stiff for front-pointing. However, there are many leather boots on the market that will handsomely meet the demands of alpine conditions. Leather boots are also lighter, which gives you more sensitivity. Make sure, however, that they have grooves which will accommodate crampons.

ICE AXE

There are many different designs of ice axe, from the standard walker's axe (called the piolet) to highly technical ice tools. For entry-level alpinists the piolet will be more than sufficient, but make sure it has a steel head. The pick should have a crescent curve with sharp teeth running the full length. Opposite the pick is the adze. This is a flat cutting blade used for chopping and scraping away ice, etc. Between the pick and the adze is a hole for threading your wrist leash. At the other end is a flat dagger-like point for pushing into the snow. The shaft could be bare metal, or lightly covered with a rubber sheath. In addition to

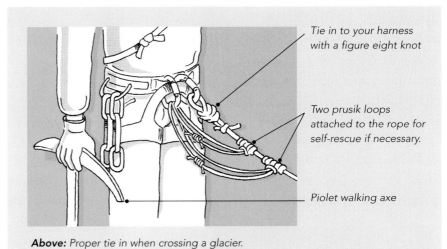

Tie in to your harness with a figure eight knot

Two prusik loops attached to the rope for self-rescue if necessary.

Piolet walking axe

Above: *Proper tie in when crossing a glacier.*

specialized snow and ice gear you will need standard mountaineering equipment like ropes, helmet, harness, assorted protection gear, and clothing suited to the climate.

USING CRAMPONS AND AN ICE AXE

The basic rule is to keep the weight on your feet. On low-angle slopes keep your crampons flat and balance over them. This is called French technique and is a very versatile and useful technique to master. Remember, always stomp your crampons into the ice. this way the points will bite. At the same time hold your axe by the head, plunging the tip of the shaft into the snow slope above you. On steeper ice you will need to use front-point technique. This is when you attack the slope front-on by kicking the front points of your crampons hard into the ice. Here a single axe can be used or twin ice tools, depending on the severity of the climbing. On extreme or vertical ice (waterfalls, for instance) you definitely need two ice tools.

Left: *French technique is useful for moving on low-angled snow and ice.*

SELF-ARREST

Any slip on relatively steep snow or ice and the self-arrest is the only thing between you and a rapidly accelerating descent. For this you will need an ice axe.

Practise on a firm snow slope that is not too steep. It must have a long run-out without boulders and no drop-off at the end. Do not wear crampons either: if any of the points snag the crisp layer of snow during your falling slide, you will be abruptly flipped over and possibly break an ankle.

Lie on your back with feet pointing down and start sliding. Wrap your right hand around the head where it joins the shaft with the pick facing out. With the other hand, grab the shaft midway down and roll over to the right to face the snow. (If you had the head of the axe in your left hand, then you should roll to the left.) Gradually insert the pick into the surface of the snow to stop your slide.

Try this on steeper slopes and also experiment with different falls.

Below: The illustration on the left shows the self-arrest technique used in the most common way of falling. The two illustrations on the right show self-arrrest technique when the climber has fallen head-first and first needs to swing the body round.

GLACIER TRAVEL

If you venture onto glaciers on a regular basis, the chances are you will fall into a crevasse. Many experienced alpinists have met their deaths this way.

Ideally, you should try to cross a glacier when there is the least amount of snow possible, which will make it easier to see the crevasses and avoid them. This is more likely to be the case during the summer months.

Try to pick a solid-looking line across a glacier, where the stress-fractures are few. Avoid areas where the glacier curves, or turns a corner, because this is where you are likely to find the most stress-fractures and crevasses.

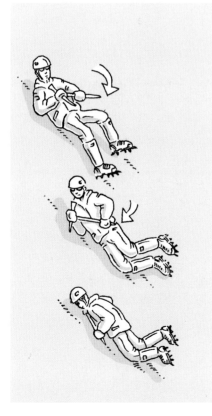

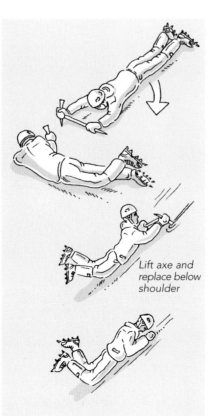

Lift axe and replace below shoulder

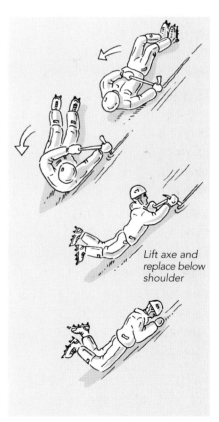

Lift axe and replace below shoulder

CROSSING AS A PARTY OF TWO

Each climber must tie into the rope (using a karabiner) about 20m (66ft) from their respective ends. The length of rope between them must be a few metres shorter than the excess rope from the climber to the end of the rope. Coil this excess rope and wear it over your shoulder. Attach two prusik loops to the rope directly in front of your harness (as if you were going to perform the standard prusik technique). Clip the other ends of the prusik loops to another karabiner on your harness.

When crossing the glacier, always try to keep the rope between you and your partner as taut as possible, since a slack rope only means a longer fall. Finding a safe path across the glacier is up to the leader. With experience you will be able to recognize trouble areas, like depressions, which are likely to hide crevasses.

If you take a wrong step and break through into a crevasse, it might be no more serious than a plunge up to the armpits, in which case you will be able to pull yourself out using the rope. If you fall deeper into the crevasse:

Step 1: Don't panic!

Step 2: Your partner will have held your fall by embedding his ice axe into the surface of the glacier.

Step 3: The loose rope is tossed down to you so that you can attach your pack to it, so that you do not have to prusik with a full pack on.

Step 4: Undo the prusiks from your

Right: Use of a rope can speed up progress over a glacier. The climbers feel confident about rescue and this can reduce lengthy detours.

Right: A typical crevasse rescue showing the Z-pulley in action.

harness and use them to prusik up the rope. If you find it awkward at the lip, use the rope to which your pack is attached to assist you.

If the climber has been hurt in the fall, then the climber on the surface should rig up a hoisting system. This is normally an assisted hoist (three-way or Z-pulley hoist).

Once the climber has been hoisted to the lip, the best way to get him over the lip, is to rig up a self-belay, go to the edge and physically haul him out.

Alpine climbing demands physical endurance. It generally involves long routes, which can sometimes take several days to complete. It is mentally taxing and often will entail some spectacular epics, like trying to climb the last few pitches in the dark, or getting storm-bound on a little ledge for days, or simply trying to survive a long and arduous route.

Start off with some short and easy alpine routes before venturing onto the bigger and more demanding peaks.

Above right: *Rongbuk and Everest. The Himalayan range attracts not only climbers, but also people seeking out the various Eastern philosophies and religions.*
Right: *In the midday heat a resupply team of Sherpa porters trudge up the Western Cwm towards Camp II. The Geneva Spur, the Lhotse Face and Lhotse itself rear up ahead of them with Nuptse North Face on the right.*

Himalayan climbing

The Himalayan mountain range is home to the biggest and most serious mountains on earth. Think of the European Alps, then treble it in height from base to summit, and spread it over an area the size of Europe. It is a magnificent and powerful mountain range that attracts climbers, trekkers, and people seeking the compelling magnetism of the various Eastern philosophies and beliefs that abound within the folds of those snowy giants.

From the first attempts to scale these lofty peaks a hundred years ago, it became evident that these peaks required different strategies to those used on the Alpine peaks. Their size, altitude and remoteness demanded siege tactics. A 6000m–8000m (20,000–26,000ft) peak could not be scaled from

base to summit and back in a matter of a few days. The objective dangers and amount of ground to be covered was just too great. This is how the traditional Himalayan expeditions began. Climbers from the West would come to the Himalaya and enlist the services of local people to help carry up huge amounts of equipment and food, which enabled them to set up a base camp at the foot of the mountain they wished to climb.

From here a series of camps would be established ever higher up the peak, until the final camp was set up at a point from where it would be possible to make a single push for the summit and return within a single day.

During the course of the expedition, which could take anything from four to twelve weeks, this series of camps would be stocked with provisions. That way teams of climbers could climb the peak (using supplemental oxygen on the higher mountains) by using these camps for replenishment and shelter.

It was soon realized that the Sherpas, from Nepal and Tibet, were exceptionally strong and outstanding mountaineers. They were used increasingly as high altitude climbers to partner the Western climbers as equals on some of the most difficult peaks. Indeed, many was the occasion that Sherpas would act as guides for their 'sahibs' and take the role of the stronger climber in the team.

All the 8000m (26,000ft) peaks in the world (all 14 of them situated in the greater Himalayan range), and most of the 7000m (23,000ft) peaks, were first climbed using these traditional expedition-style tactics.

Expedition tactics are still being used today on many of the bigger peaks. Many of these are commercial trips, with clients being guided by mountaineers for substantial sums of money.

Over the last 20 to 30 years, world-class mountaineers have been looking for new challenges in the Himalayas, now that all the main peaks had been climbed.

The next obvious step was to attempt these giants with alpine tactics and without supplemental

Above: *The highest mountain in the world, Mount Everest, was originally conquered with Himalayan siege tactics and is still climbed in that manner, although many climbers have now climbed it alpine-style and without supplementary oxygen.*

oxygen. They still employ Sherpas and porters (though fewer) to ferry supplies to base camp, but from here the game changes dramatically. Climbers would set off for the summit in an attempt to do the entire climb in a single push. They carry all their food, equipment and a tent with them; setting up and breaking camp along the way. The idea is to wait for a stable weather window, and then make a quick, light attempt. The boundaries of Himalayan climbing (as with all other forms of climbing) are being pushed out further and further all the time, as modern mountaineers seek ever greater challenges.

Many Himalayan peaks have now been climbed alpine-style without oxygen. Some of the 8000m (26,000ft) giants have even been soloed. Winter ascents of some of the difficult peaks are also being attempted. Even speed-ascent records of Mount Everest are being broken every year, currently under 11 hours from Base Camp to summit. Himalayan climbing has come a long way from the days of Albert Mummery, who disappeared on Nanga Parbat in 1895 and the Duke of Abruzzi whose name is inextricably linked to K2, regarded by many to be the most difficult mountain on earth to climb.

Right: Climbing on Nanga Parbat in the Punjab Himalayas.

ICE AND WATERFALLS

The ever changing medium of ice and frozen waterfalls throws many a challenge at the climber. In countries like Canada, Scotland and Norway the winter season almost always guarantees the formation of spectacular ice pillars, slender ice ribbons and frozen couloirs that offer steep and exciting climbing.

The attraction

While frontpointing up a steep slope or slowly making your way up a bulging pillar, you will be faced with rotten ice, long run-outs, freezing temperatures and saturating conditions. It can be a terrifying experience that will have many a non-believer praying for a second chance. But you will be back for more. You will be back to feel that solid 'kathunk' as the tips of your ice tools cleave into the crisp early morning ice; feel the points of your crampons biting deep as you gingerly weave your way through spectacular chande-lier formations; feel the satisfaction of placing a solid ice screw; see your breath collide with the icy air and form little icicles around your mouth; and feel that raw passion as you top out over the lip of a spectacular ice pillar in a winter wonderland of frozen beauty.

There will also be times when you will be saying to yourself 'If I make this route, that's it. I'll sell my ice gear and stick to warm, solid rock. No more death defying ice epics.' Fortunately, it seems, the human brain is better at remem-bering the good things in life than the bad, scary stuff. So, as much as you will swear to a safer life from now on, you will soon find yourself sharpening your tools for the next ice trip.

Left: *A climber showing good technique while climbing a frozen waterfall.*

Equipment

ICE TOOLS

The ice tools used for water ice are very different from the ones used on snowy mountains. Instead of a straight-shafted piolet, you use technical axes with bent shafts: one with an adze for chopping and scrapping, and one with a hammer for pounding. Tool heads must be interchangeable so that broken heads can be replaced and pick designs can be switched to accommodate different ice conditions. Stick to one brand. This way the feel of both axes will be similar and your spare heads will fit either tool.

Crampons: Like rock climbing, footwork plays a vital role in ice climbing. It maintains good balance and keeps the weight off your arms. Crampons come in two styles – flexible and rigid. For steep ice, rigid crampons are best. You will feel more solid and get more precision in your footwork. When buying crampons, make sure they fit solidly on your boots. You will want the clip-on style, as opposed to the strap-on ones, for steep ice. Check that the metal bindings on the crampons match the shape of the front and back of your boot. If you are climbing hard water-ice, choose vertical, serrated frontpoints over horizontal flat ones, since these slice and bite into frozen, brittle ice more easily and cleanly.

Boots: Although the trend is back to leather boots for general mountaineering, plastic boots are still the way to go for steep ice and waterfalls. They are waterproof, warm, insulated and absolutely rigid, with stiff uppers that will lock your foot in place for solid frontpointing. Make sure that the crampon grooves on the boot are deep enough to accept the metal bindings on the crampons securely.

Get snug-fitting boots that do not squeeze your foot. In cold conditions good blood circulation helps to keep your feet warm. A boot that squeezes your foot will hamper circulation and result in frozen digits. Remember, plastics do not stretch, so buy them the correct size.

Gloves: Mittens are generally warmer than gloves, because your fingers are touching and can share their body heat. In a glove they are each in separate little compartments; having to fend for

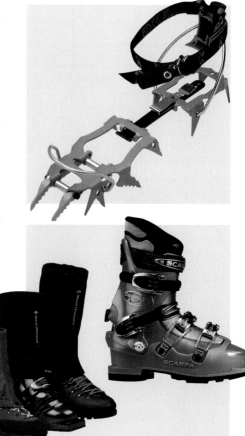

Fully adjustable and interchangeable head

Hammer head for driving in ice screws.

Serrated and down-pointing pick for greater purchase.

Wrist leash

Wrist loop

Flat pointed shaft tip for plunging into snow surface.

From the top: Essential ice climbing gear: ice axe; crampons; and specially designed boots, fully compatible with all crampons, with high gaiters to keep the feet dry.

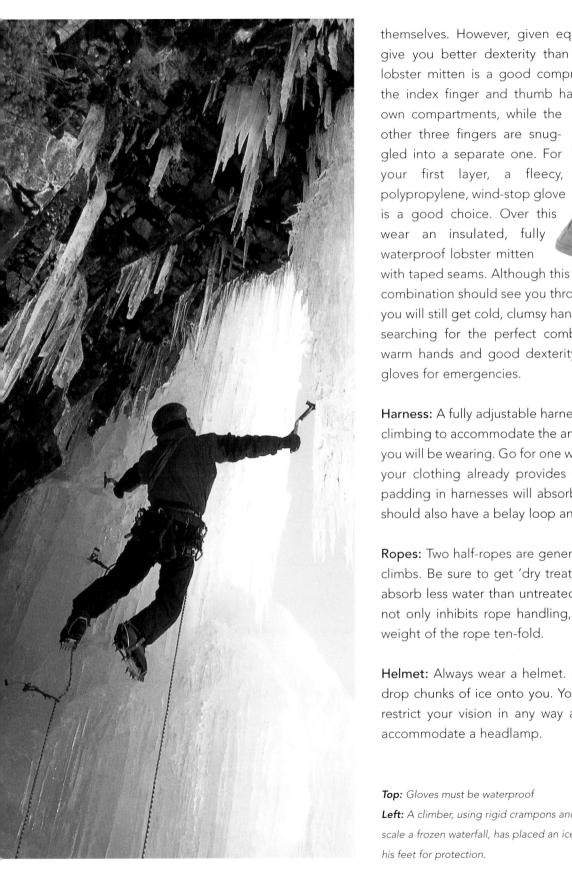

themselves. However, given equal thickness, gloves give you better dexterity than mittens. The lobster mitten is a good compromise, with the index finger and thumb having their own compartments, while the other three fingers are snuggled into a separate one. For your first layer, a fleecy, polypropylene, wind-stop glove is a good choice. Over this wear an insulated, fully waterproof lobster mitten with taped seams. Although this combination should see you through most conditions, you will still get cold, clumsy hands and will forever be searching for the perfect combination to give you warm hands and good dexterity. Always carry spare gloves for emergencies.

Harness: A fully adjustable harness is necessary for ice climbing to accommodate the amount of clothing that you will be wearing. Go for one without padding, since your clothing already provides ample padding, and padding in harnesses will absorb water. Your harness should also have a belay loop and four gear loops.

Ropes: Two half-ropes are generally used on most ice climbs. Be sure to get 'dry treated' ropes, since they absorb less water than untreated ones. A soggy rope not only inhibits rope handling, it also increases the weight of the rope ten-fold.

Helmet: Always wear a helmet. Ice routes continually drop chunks of ice onto you. Your helmet should not restrict your vision in any way and must be able to accommodate a headlamp.

Top: *Gloves must be waterproof*
Left: *A climber, using rigid crampons and technical axes to scale a frozen waterfall, has placed an ice screw just beneath his feet for protection.*

Protection gear

On many ice routes you will find opportunities to place conventional rock climbing gear in rock next to the ice, so always take a selection of rock gear, depending on the route you are doing. This may also include a selection of pitons. You will need a selection of ice screws and hammer-ins, and other assorted gear like ice hooks, pickets and deadmen, again depending on the type of route you are intending to climb.

PLACING SCREWS AND HAMMER-INS

Before venturing out on your first lead, practise placing a few screws and hammer-ins while your feet are planted firmly on the ground. Try placing gear with one hand, since you will often have no choice once up on vertical ice.

Step 1. Scrape away any soft, rotten or fractured ice with the adze on your axe, until you get to a solid, uniform surface.

Step 2. Gouge a hole about two centimetres deep, angled slightly down, with the pick of your axe.

Step 3. Select a piece and firmly stab it into the pilot hole.

Step 4. Screw or hammer it in, ensuring the piece points down at about 10° to 15°. There should be solid resistance while screwing or hammering in the piece. Any variation means a difference in the compactness of the ice. Remember that an ice placement is only as solid as the ice holding it.

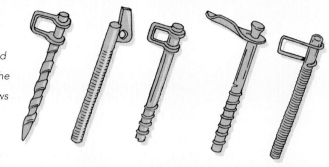

Right: An ice screw with broad threads needs to be screwed into the ice, while the finer threaded screws are hammered in. (See p47 for more modern ice screws.)

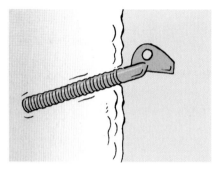

Above: The ice screw should point down by about 10–15°.

Below: A wrist leash secures a dropped tool, helps in the work of swinging the tools and lets you rest your grip by hanging your weight from it.

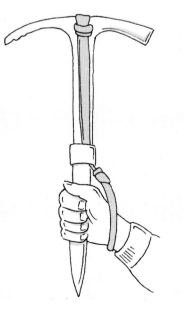

Technique

Ice climbing demands a confident approach, which only comes with plenty of practice. This involves top-roping many practice pitches; following an experienced leader on various types of ice; and experiencing a variety of angles.

Ice bouldering is an excellent way of finding your feet and to learn how to move efficiently with axe and crampons. You will learn the limits of your axes and the angles you can pull on them. Experiment with placing your crampons until you feel comfortable. Experienced ice climbers move confidently and deliberately. They place ice axes and crampons with a minimum of whacks and climb with little apparent effort.

Good axe and crampon technique, and the ability to place solid protection, are essential for enjoyable ice climbing. There are many other nuances that need to be fed into the engram (see p171) vaults of the brain, but these will be gathered as your ice climbing experience broadens.

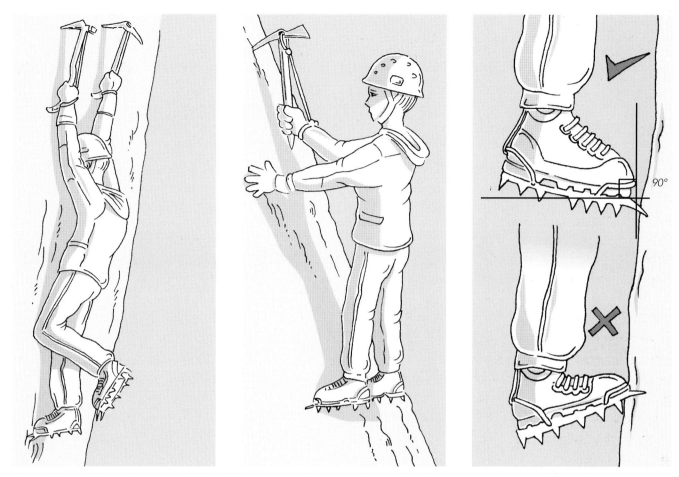

Above: *Frontpointing with two axes (left) and frontpointing with one axe (centre). The illustration on the top right shows the correct angle when frontpointing. Avoid letting your heel drop or standing on tip toe.*

SWINGING YOUR AXE

Step 1. Your grip on the shaft should be firm, but if you grip too hard your arms will tire quickly.

Step 2. Find the best strike point in the ice, where the pick will find good purchase. This takes experience, but after a while your eye will be able to recognize good placement spots.

Step 3. Concentrating on the spot chosen, swing your axe with precision and with the same force as you would use to drive a nail.

Step 4. Try not to overdrive your tools, because this will make removal difficult and tire you out unnecessarily. Here, again, experience will teach you to trust shallow placements, depending on ice conditions.

FRONTPOINTING

Step 1. Frontpointing tires your calf muscles very quickly, so make sure that your boots fit well and that your laces are tight.

Step 2. Concentrate on the angle of your kick. The crampon should be angled slightly downward (your heel should be slightly higher than your toes), to acquire good purchase. Try not to drop your heels when you get tired.

Step 3. Look at the spot where you want to place your frontpoints. Pick a spot and kick firmly and deliberately. Never reach so far up and get so stretched out that it becomes difficult for you to look down and see your feet.

Step 4. Always kick in above little bulges or ledges. This will give more support to the underside of your crampons.

PREPARATION AND TRAINING

Rock climbing puts the human body under severe stress loads. Often a climber's weight has to be supported by only the fingertips of one hand, and on occasions sometimes only one finger. This puts an enormous amount of strain on the tendons, muscles and joints. Warming up before you launch yourself onto a crimp fest or a steep and strenuous climb is imperative if you want to avoid injuries. It also primes your body for what you are about to put it through.

Warming up

If you step onto a steep route with cold muscles and tendons, it will not be long before your muscles rebel and you pump out (see glossary), making it impossible to hold onto even the biggest holds. This is called a flash pump and it is something that you should avoid. Besides turning you into a useless sack of potatoes, recovery can take a long time and you probably will not be able to reach your peak for the rest of the day.

Many climbers fail on a route for lack of (or inadequate) warming up. A good warm-up will not stop your muscles from getting pumped, but they will recover more quickly than cold ones.

You need to warm up not only those muscles that are going to support your weight, or pull you up a steep wall, but your whole body. Then you need to concentrate on high-impact areas such as fingers, forearms, elbows and shoulders. Hips are also put under a lot of strain by wide stemming moves.

A good start would be to work up a light sweat. This could be achieved by simply walking up to the crag. If the crag is one of those roadside jobs, then a short brisk walk or jog for 10 minutes will do the trick. This will give your muscles an overall gentle warm-up and prepare them for the more rigorous warm-up to come. On the way to the crag, push some finger putty for about 10 to 15 minutes.

The 'sun salutation' sequence from yoga is ideal for warming up, because it uses most of your muscle groups.

Your fingers work really hard when you are trying to scrape your way up a route, so they need a lot of attention in the warm-up process.

Your next step should be some light stretching. Remember never to stretch cold. I find that the yoga 'sun salutation' sequence is ideal for this and encompasses practically all your muscle groups. Basic yoga is not difficult and many of the opening sequences are easy to remember. Obviously, the more you do it the easier it becomes.

Start by simply standing straight and reaching up as high as you can with outstretched arms. Then, keeping your legs straight (but the knees soft – slightly bent), bend at the waist and let your upper body hang down so that your hands are touching your toes. If you can't touch your toes, don't force it. Just let your body weight pull your torso down. Hang like that for a while and then try reaching lower with your hands without straining your back. Do this a few times to stretch the ham strings in the back of your thighs and to loosen up your back muscles. Now you are ready to move into more specific warm-up exercises.

Above: *Warm up your fingers by kneading finger putty for about ten minutes.*

Stretching sequence

Stretches should be done gently for 30 seconds each. Repeat the sequence twice:

a) Stretch the forearms.

b) Stretch the intrinsic muscles of your hand by bending the first and second joints of your fingers and then stretching the third joint

c) Stretch the back of the forearms by twisting your arm out and then pulling up the back of the hand.

d) Stretch the inside of the forearm and the tendon at the inside of the elbow by pushing your inverted hand flat against a flat surface.

e) Stretch the latissimus dorsi by lifting your arms above your head and then leaning over to each side.

f) Stretch the hamstring by sitting with one leg bent and one leg straight. Lean forward, keeping your back straight.

g) Stretch the groin muscles by stepping up onto a boulder and rocking forward.

h) Stretch the calves by pushing against a wall.

i) Stretch the neck by gently pulling to one side at a time.

j) Shoulder helicopters. Lean forward and spin your arms around your shoulders with bent arms – forward and backwards 20 times – not too fast! Then slowly move your straight arms forward and backwards to the limit for 20 repetitions – feel your back and chest stretching. Some climbers have very lax shoulders and should be really careful when stretching shoulders: you should move into the stretch slowly and stop at the first sign of discomfort.

k) Crimping can lead to injuries so, before you start pulling hard on tiny edges, grab a crimp on the ground for about 10 seconds and then release. Repeat two or three times, increasing the crimp force.

After this sequence you should be ready and psyched to jump onto the rock and crank some routes. Your first route or two of the day should be easy ones, well within your grade; routes with reasonable

STRETCH THE FOREARMS

LATISSIMUS DORSI STRETCH

STRETCH THE MUSCLES ON THE INSIDE OF THE SHOULDER

STRETCH THE INSIDE OF THE FOREARM AND THE TENDON AT THE INSIDE OF THE ELBOW

holds that will not over-tax your body.

The first route should just bring some blood to your forearms and the second route should give you a mild pump. How-ever, crags rarely conform to rigid grading require-ments, so you will have to adapt accordingly.

Ensure that after a long lunch break you are still warm. If not, then go through a few exercises to loosen up before you start climbing again. Stretching at the end of the day is also important for keeping you supple and injury-free. It is a good idea, and also fun, to end a climbing ses-sion with a few easy routes and a simple stretching routine.

HAMSTRING STRETCH

GROIN STRETCH

CALF STRETCH

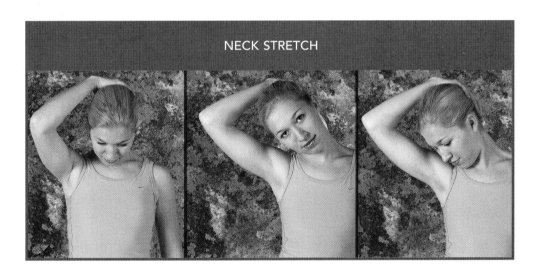

NECK STRETCH

SHOULDER HELICOPTERS

WARMING UP ON CRIMPS

Mental preparation

A short distance off the ground, it becomes evident that your mind plays an important role in climbing. A strong mind will improve your performance and increase the enjoyment and fun factor exponentially. You need to get your mind to toe the line.

Some people have a very high fear threshold, while others get gripped by fear easily – and for no apparent reason other than having fresh air under their feet.

It is important that you understand and trust the rope and equipment, and the way the equipment is used to protect you and your party during a rock climb.

For instance, if you are leading a pitch that is pushing your ability somewhat and you find yourself 2m (7ft) above a solid piece of gear, faced with a tricky move – and you have little faith in the system, you will find it almost impossible to push through the move. On the other hand, if you believe that the piece will hold your fall, then your mind will allow you to carry on. This doesn't mean that you won't be scared. Of course you will. It is only natural to be scared if you are 50m (164ft) off the deck and face a potential 6m (20ft) fall. There is no climber alive who would boast of feeling no fear at all. Fear keeps you alive. It is a healthy part of climbing. It forces you to double-check your harness and tie-in knot, to check gear placements, and it prevents you

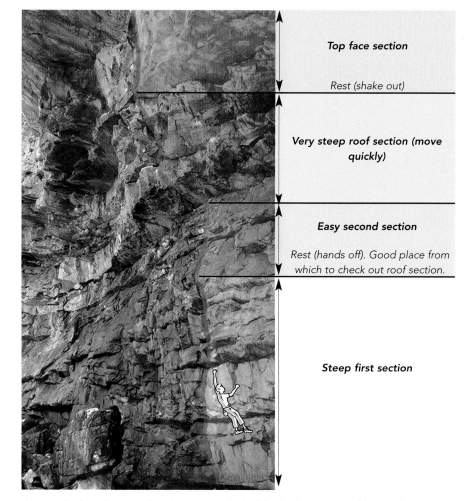

Above: Analyze the route: break it up into climbable chunks, separated by good rest spots. Then take each section between the rests and visualize them as individual moves.

from doing stupid things. The trick is to control your fear so that you can continue to behave rationally and climb smoothly and prevent it from paralysing you.

There is a definite link between mental strength and physical ability. If you attempt a climb at your limit after a period of absence from the crag, your mind will be throwing all sorts of doubts around, like: 'Will I have enough endurance to hang in on that steep section' or 'Will I be able to

fiddle in that nut at the crux while hanging off the two-finger pocket?' On the other hand, if you attempt the route well prepared, strong and firing on all cylinders, your mind will be relaxed, your climbing will be smoother and, overall, you will be confident and have more fun.

MIND CONTROL

Any preparation you do will help your mind shut the doors on doubt.
1) **Warming up.** This is your first

Above: *To overcome your fear, you need to believe in the system: that the ropes, your knots and the gear placements will hold when you fall.*

maintain mental focus. In this, too, yoga is an important aid in climbing. Besides allowing you to work through a beneficial series of warm-up exercises and stretches, it also teaches you focus and mind control. After six months of practising yoga my confidence and mind control increased dramatically – as did my climbing ability. Remember: the body cannot go where the mind has not already travelled.

MENTAL FOCUS

When climbing, your mind is generally concentrating on the job in hand, but there can be many distractions: people chatting or shouting at the base of the crag; a climber on the route next to you grunting, or even falling off. Being able to narrow and maintain focus is an invaluable mental skill. When approaching a crux sequence, or about to launch into it, every move must be precisely calculated; your mind concentrating on every micro move; your breathing deep and steady, drawing strength from your inner core. You hear no sound and see nothing but the immediate rock around you. Each finger placement and toe hold, no matter what size or shape, is measured by the eye, calculated by the brain, and an appropriate movement executed by the body, with balance always kept in check. It requires precision. This type of mental focus, combined with solid physical strength and ability, will get your grades soaring.

step to mind control because a warmed-up body feels more confident and in control.

2) **Relaxing.** Block out thoughts not related to climbing. Close your eyes, breathe deeply, and visualize yourself climbing confidently, smoothly and in control.

3) **Visualize the route.** Look at the route. Try to visualize yourself executing the moves. Know where the rest spots are and where the gear placements and cruxes are.

4) **Stay calm.** When you start the route talk to yourself. Tell yourself to stay calm, to relax. Try and keep your arms as fresh as possible on the route. Pumped arms will lead to a pumped brain and a pumped brain only means trouble.

5) **Remember to breathe.** It is not uncommon to stop breathing while trying to execute a crux sequence. This only stops valuable oxygen from been pumped to your screaming muscles. Deep, continuous breathing also helps to

FEAR OF FALLING

No one likes falling. In fact it is not the fall that is scary, it is the feeling that you are about to fall that is scary, or not knowing what the fall is going to be like.

If you are climbing a steep bolted route that is a little run out and you are getting a bit pumped as you get near the top, your mind will start playing tricks on you. You will be reluctant to leave the security of a bolt to venture into 'run-out country'; not knowing if your pumped forearms will last until the next clip. Your mind will be firing all sorts of questions: 'What happens if you get to the next bolt and you can't hold on long enough to clip it?' or, worse still: 'What if you pull up slack to clip, then lose it before you actually clip, leaving you to face a whipper of mega proportions?'

Most of the time you will end up hanging on the previous bolt to recoup your strength, before continuing. Nine times out of ten you would have made the next bolt and even get the red point (see glossary), but the ever-powerful mind always has the last word.

The fear of falling is irrational: what can be safer than falling on an overhanging bolted route high above the ground? You're not going to hit anything and the gear is not going to rip.

To come to terms with falling, set yourself up on a steep route with the last bolt at your knees and jump off. Then climb back up and

Above: *Each finger placement and toe hold, no matter what size or shape, is measured by the eye, calculated by the brain, and an appropriate movement is executed by the body.*

repeat the jump, this time with the bolt at your feet. Continue this until you have taken falls of up to 5m (16ft) – or longer if you start enjoying it! Once you have the fear of falling under control, you will be able to push yourself to the limit with pumped arms, often slipping success into the bag.

Advanced training

Training is associated with blood, sweat and tears, and many dedicated climbers train up to 20 hours or more a week. Advanced training will make you fiercely strong, give you confidence, build engrams (see p171) and, most of all, give you satisfaction and fun. American climber Dale Goddard states in his book *Performance Rock Climbing* that

'Climbing is a movement sport', and Wolfgang Gullich, the late German rock star said 'Strength only supplements good technique!'

So why did we spend so much of our time in the early 1990s hanging off finger boards, pumping iron and trying to outdo one another in one-arm pull-up games? Because we had got it all wrong! Watch children who start climbing young. At first they must rely on good technique to pull them through those tricky sequences. Then they develop strength, and the subsequent combination of technique and strength is phenomenal!

Opposite: *Practise falling to help overcome your fears.*

The current trend is to train those two aspects together: movement and strength. And we make sure that we always have fun at the climbing wall.

The goals in training are: perfecting movement, building strength and endurance, preventing injury and cultivating the hunger to succeed.

If you want to build up a high level of strength and endurance that will peak at, and last through, a competition; or a day trying to red-point a hard project; or a longer trip to try some hard routes, you need a training cycle. A good training cycle is usually three months, but try to keep it between two and four months. To prevent injury you must rest for 10% of your cycle (see graph).

STRENGTH TRAINING

There are four types of strength training: aerobic energy restoration and capillarity (ARC); hypertrophy (HYP); recruitment (REC); and power endurance (PE).

1. Aerobic Energy Restoration and Capillarity [ARC] (weeks 1–2). Imagine taking a lengthy break from climbing and then jumping onto a campus board. Your muscles will have weakened and a betting man will place money on the odds of you hurting yourself!

So, for weeks 1 and 2 of your cycle you should do ARC training, which consists of climbing continuously for 30 to 45 minutes at about 20% of your maximum strength. The aim is to teach the muscles to adapt to high demands for aerobic energy restoration by loading

them at a low density, long duration that is continuous (no breaks for 30 to 45 minutes). Train on a vertical to gently overhanging wall, trying to keep a mild pump in your arms. Rest for the same length of time, before doing another set. If you get a burning pump, get off the wall for a minute or two before continuing at a milder pace.

During that 30–45 minute period you will have executed about 360 moves. Many of those are repeats, which your body will store as engrams. This is particularly useful in competitions and other on-sight situations. Your body is also adjusting to the training and will react by slowly getting stronger.

Physiologically speaking, when you get pumped the capillaries in your forearms are squeezed shut,

MAXIMUM STRENGTH

A muscle consists of thousands of muscle fibres that are either 'on' or 'off'. When pulling at 20% of your maximum strength, 20% of these fibres will be on. Doing super-hard boulder problems or campus boarding (see glossary) at maximum strength will recruit 100% of these fibres.

Right: Overall Performance Improvement after one training cycle. This also shows how volume of training changes over the cycle.

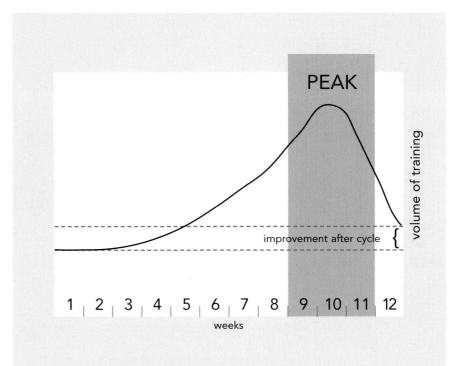

restricting the flow of blood needed to supply oxygen and remove the byproducts of energy metabolism. When you do ARC training, more capillaries will gradually develop, and your blood will have more highways along which to travel, bringing oxygen and removing by-products!

The down side of this training is that it is difficult to hold back and climb at 20% of your capacity for more than 30 minutes. Nevertheless it could be the key to your success, so psyche up, grab a friend to train with, get some music going, and get mildly pumped! You can do up to three days of ARC training in a row, since your muscles won't get too fatigued, but remember to listen to your body, and don't ignore it when it complains. Even though you aren't climbing continuously, all that easy climbing is good for light endurance and engrams. For the rest of your cycle try to do some ARC training once a week to keep up your aerobic energy restoration and capillarity.

2. Hypertrophy (weeks 3–7)

Now that you have adjusted your muscles after two weeks of ARC you'll want to build some power. The plan is to build the muscles in the upper body, particularly in the forearms. For this kind of exercise you should train at about 60–80% of maximum strength for 6–12 moves on a climbing wall. Longish boulder problems are ideal for this kind of training. Do about 30 boulder problems over 3–4 hours. During the first two hypertrophy sessions you will feel weak, but soon after that your body will adjust and you will start cranking hard boulder problems.

If you take climbing seriously, get your own gym. It allows you to train at any time and – more importantly – no one will change your set problems. Set problems are particularly important in the hypertrophy and power endurance phases, because they allow you to do large volumes of climbing, which is essential for competitions and on-sighting. You will do the problems first go, without wasting time trying to figure them out.

All your problems should be documented. Letter every panel, and number the holds on each panel. Then use a spreadsheet to mark the problems.

Various sports require you to develop engrams, or patterns of movement.

ENGRAMS

This is the way in which movements are stored in the brain. When you climb, your body learns to recognize certain patterns and stores them in the brain as engrams. The more you climb, the more engrams you acquire, and the more you repeat a move, the more ingrained an existing engram becomes.

You will find that even after a long break you will still be able to climb, with relative ease, a route that you know really well. However, a similarly graded route that is unfamiliar to you, will seem desperately difficult! That's engrams in action. They allow you to recognize problems quickly and your body reacts to these so that you flow through the different sequences easily.

What you are aiming for in this phase is not to get pumped, but to keep going until you fall off the wall because you can't pull another move due to lack of power. After 2–3 hours of good hypertrophy training your muscles should ache, and the next morning you should feel that you have been through a hard training session. It is not advisable to do two days of hypertrophy training in a row. You can alternate days of hypertrophy training with ARC or easy climbing, but always remember to rest the day before your next session of hypertrophy, so that you are fresh enough to pull hard.

Try not to repeat problems in one training session because variety will ensure that you enjoy your training. A motivated training partner will also help you to get the most out of each session and uncover your weaknesses as you struggle to climb your partner's type of problems.

On the weekend, you should get out and do some hard bouldering; short, powerful routes; or easy ARC routes. This ensures that you won't fade away in your gym. Remember to do some climbing outdoors, since it will keep your mind in touch with leading routes.

Right: Training Type Breakdown. This shows how to manage the volume of training for each type of training over the cycle.

3. Recruitment (week 8)

Huge amounts of power are not necessary for competitions and long routes, but an increase in strength will equate to an increase in endurance, since you won't be pulling so hard (but using smaller percentage of your maximum strength) when you use that sloper or edge. To crank really hard you need to teach your muscles to use 100% of your muscle fibres.

We teach our muscle fibres to all pull at once (100% recruitment) by pulling real hard and real simple! During weeks 6–7 you should have started doing some short, hard problems in the middle of your hypertrophy sessions. During week 8 do progressively harder problems for about 45 minutes. Then follow this with about 45 minutes of intense campus boarding (see opposite). The campus boarding sets should last no longer than 5 seconds, and must concentrate on your forearms. You should focus yourself mentally, since it is no easy task doing recruitment training. After this session, cool down by doing problems that don't tax the same areas as short, hard problems with small holds, until your forearms ache.

Again, listen to your body, but a hard recruitment session may need to be followed by two days of rest. A boulderer, or a climber who concentrates on short, hard redpoints, should spend more time on recruitment to improve their strength. A climber who concentrates on competitions or on-sighting will want to develop engrams rather than strength, so will want to do more moves and less recruitment.

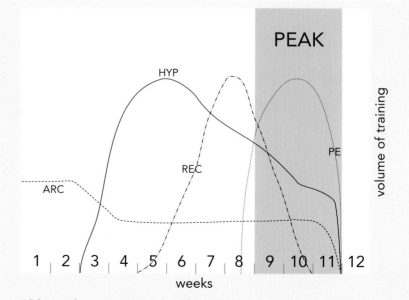

ARC – aerobic restoration and capillarity; HYP – hypertrophy; REC –recruitment; PE – power endurance

4. Power Endurance (weeks 9–11)

This is the training that masochistic climbers love so much. The saying 'no pain, no gain' applies here. The idea is to get so pumped that you won't be able to brush your teeth before collapsing into bed.

Climb a set problem of 25 to 30 moves (made by linking three or four hypertrophy problems). Then rest for about 3 minutes before doing another, different set of 25 to 30 moves. The idea is not to get too exhausted in the first two sets, but to pace yourself. Rest for 3 minutes, and then, finally, exhaust yourself on a different problem. This should be about the same intensity as the first two, but try to link up about 40 to 50 very difficult ('pumpy') moves. Rest for about 30 minutes and repeat the triple set until your heart rate goes up. By the end of the evening you should be so exhausted that you can't even do your warm-up problems.

It is important to keep in mind that you are now on the verge of overtraining, so you should limit the length of this cycle to three weeks. Listen to your body and watch out for those aches.

Power endurance (PE) training shows benefits very quickly, and after two or three sessions you will feel your endurance start to sky-rocket. After the first week, get out to the crags and start pushing your previous limits for on-sight climbing, or try that steep and difficult red-point, since these are also good forms of PE training.

Organize your training so that you will have done about two weeks of PE and 'pumpy' rock climbing before a competition.

There is one unfortunate trade-off with this phase of training, and that is that it can lower your power. To combat this, spend half an evening doing recruitment exercises and then finish off with two or three triple power endurance sets. This will ensure that your power levels remain high.

5. Rest (week 12)

This is essential for injury prevention. Rest for two weeks. Whatever you do, don't climb! You need to be psyched and well rested when you start your cycle again.

With all training it is vital to warm up properly before each session and do some stretching and warm-down exercises after the session.

Climbing injury

Climbing injuries refer to those sustained due to the strain exerted on the muscles, tendons and joints and not to wounds caused by sharp rock or impact.

Few climbers can boast an injury-free career. Pulled tendons, torn muscles and aching joints are very much part of a climber's life.

Right: A campus board is placed at an overhanging angle against a wall. Hand holds, mounted on the board, are used to do pull-ups by 'walking' up the rungs. Avoid climbing down, since it can cause inner elbow injury.

INJURY PREVENTION

Warm up. The best way to prevent injury is to warm up before every training or climbing session and to warm down and stretch well afterwards. Failing to warm up properly puts you at risk of pulling a tendon or tearing a muscle.

Rest days. Overuse of muscles and tendons also leads to injuries. For that reason you must have rest days on a road trip when you are climbing continually for two or three weeks. Depending on the type and severity of the climbing you should have a complete rest day after two days of climbing. This means no climbing at all, not even very easy ones. This gives your body time to recover.

On a particularly intense climbing routine it is advisable to rest on alternate days, or even to take two days off. The important thing is to listen to your body. If

your elbows start to throb, or a finger starts to ache, then stop climbing; rest a few days; perhaps have some physiotherapy; and make sure the problem is solved before you start climbing again. Climbing with achy muscles or tendons is a one way ticket to a long lay-off.

ANTAGONISTIC EXERCISES

Climbers tend to use certain muscles in very definite patterns. This increases the strength (and size) of a muscle group (affecting length and tightness) more than that of an opposing muscle group.

Climbers tend to suffer from a high incidence of shoulder problems. This is mainly due to the anterior deltoid being more developed than the posterior deltoid. To prevent this, antagonistic exercises should be performed to strengthen the posterior deltoid.

Enrolling in Pilates, stretch or yoga classes is a good way of learning how to do the exercises necessary to ensure balanced muscle development.

TYPES OF INJURIES AND TREATMENT:
FINGERS

An increasingly common climbing injury is the pulled or torn A2 pulley on the middle or ring finger tendon. The pulley is the little band that keeps the tendon close to the bone between the middle knuckle and the hand. When the tendon is over-strained it pulls hard against this pulley, thereby tearing it.

The only treatment is complete rest. You should not climb at all for a few weeks, depending on the severity of the injury. During the first week or so, use ice on the injury (see Treating overuse injuries opposite) and take anti-inflammatory medicines. Once the pain and swelling are gone, rest for a few more weeks, then do some gentle exercises, like playing with finger putty. Begin climbing on easy routes with large holds, then progress gradually to steeper routes, but try to keep away from small holds. When you start climbing again always use finger tape to reinforce the injured finger.

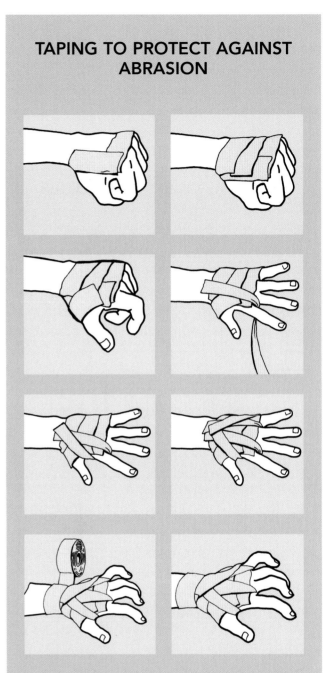

TAPING TO PROTECT AGAINST ABRASION

Dry the hands and ensure that the tape adheres properly at each stage. Layer tape over the back of the hand, fold non-elastic tape sticky-side-out between the fingers, and avoid taping the palm. An additional band around the wrist may be necessary to keep the tape in place.

ELBOWS

There is no such term as climber's elbow, but unfortunately climbers can be inflicted with tennis elbow and golfer's elbow. Tennis elbow is the inflammation of the tendon on the outside of the elbow in the middle of the joint and golfer's elbow is the inflammation of the tendon where it joins the elbow on the inside, below the knob. Both injuries are commonly caused by overuse and can persist for a long time, taking many weeks of rest to heal. Physiotherapy does help, but you will need a lot of patience. The other course of action is the use of cortisone. This is frowned upon by many, and for good reason, but for these type of injuries it has a high success rate. An opinion from a relevant medical specialist won't do any harm. Once on the mend, antagonistic exercises can speed up healing and reduce the likelihood of a recurrence.

SHOULDERS

The shoulder is a very complex joint, and due to the high loads and leverage that climbing puts on the shoulder, it can be injured fairly easily. The most common injuries affect the rotator cuff and, to a lesser degree, the acromioclavicular joint (AC joint). Both are serious injuries and should be treated by a professional immediately.

Complete rest is a prerequisite for healing and if you are lucky you will get away with some physiotherapy. If you're unlucky, you could be looking at cortisone shots, or surgery. Here again, antagonistic exercises can speed up healing and help prevent recurrence.

TREATING OVERUSE INJURIES

The four steps, remembered by the acronym RICE, are rest, ice, compression and elevation

• Rest. Avoid the activity that caused the injury and any another action that causes pain or swelling. Pay attention to aches and pains. Exercising before an injury has healed can worsen it and increase the chance of recurrence. Rest is needed for repair. Rest an injury until it is pain free.

• Ice. Ice is the most effective, safest, and cheapest first aid treatment for injuries. It should be applied as soon as possible for 10 to 30 minutes at a time, intermittently, for 48 to 72 hours. It relieves the pain and reduces the swelling and tissue damage and speeds the repair process. Protect your skin from the direct application of ice and do not ice the injury for more than 30 minutes at a time.

• Compression. A compression bandage helps to reduce the amount of swelling and loss of motion. Be careful not to apply the bandage too tightly. The bandage is meant to reduce swelling, not impair blood flow to the injury.

• Elevation. Elevate the injured limb above the level of your heart. Elevation reduces swelling at the injury site.

• Seek medical care if your injury appears more serious than a mild overuse injury. In the meantime, follow the RICE steps. They will relieve pain and prevent further damage. Also seek medical care for injuries to joints and any other injury that does not get better with home care within 10 days.

THE SHOULDER JOINT

The shoulder joint is formed at the junction of three bones: the collarbone (clavicle), the shoulder blade (scapula), and the arm bone (humerus). The scapula and clavicle form the socket of the joint, and the humerus has a round head that fits within this socket. The end of the scapula is called the acromion, and the joint between this part of the scapula and clavicle is called the acromioclavicular joint.

EMERGENCY PROCEDURES

In rock climbing, alpine or Himalayan climbing there is always an element of risk. The greater the climb the greater the risk. In most cases these risks can be kept to acceptable levels through experience (being able to read mountain and weather conditions) and good planning. The third, and very important, ingredient is luck. Many climbers will never be involved in an accident, or an emergency situation, but if you are, then knowledge of emergency procedures can prevent a minor mishap from turning into a nightmare.

No two mountains, climbs, pitches or situations are the same. It is rare that you will use exactly the same emergency procedures on two separate occasions. You need to know the basic techniques and then improvise according to the situation

To learn everything connected to the procedures involved in emergencies would take a great deal of time and dedication. The theory could fill a book on its own. In this chapter we look at some of the basic ways of extricating yourself from tricky situations.

On a mountain you will not have an abundance of equipment, but only the gear necessary for the climb itself. However, one piece of gear that you should never leave home without is a set of prusik loops. These innocuous-looking pieces of cord weigh hardly anything, but are invaluable. (See p80, 99, 100.)

Locking off

In order to free both hands during belaying or abseiling, while the rope is still under tension, the rope has to be locked off. This can be achieved in various ways. The simplest method is to wrap the rope around your thigh two or three times. This is effective, but uncomfortable and should only be used for brief periods.

BELAY PLATES AND FIGURE EIGHT DESCENDERS

There are a number of ways to lock off with the use of belay plates and figure eight descenders. The best of these methods rely on a hitch which can be tied or untied while there is a load on one end of the rope (the live rope). Push a bight of rope from the dead end (rope that's not under tension) through your locking karabiner. Then take another bight of rope and push it through the loop of the previous bight. This will trap the rope when released and stop it from running. For double security it is best to back this up with another half hitch around the karabiner.

With any belay plate a safe lock-off can also be made by tying a knot in the dead end of the rope and letting it lock up against the plate. It can be difficult to undo under load, but is nevertheless handy to protect a partner when swapping gear, etc., at a belay stance.

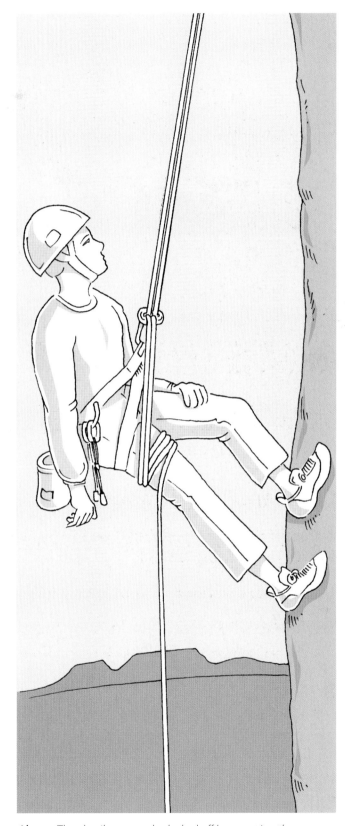

Above: *The abseil rope can be locked off by wrapping the rope around a thigh. It is uncomfortable and a short-term solution only.*

LOCKING OFF A BELAY PLATE

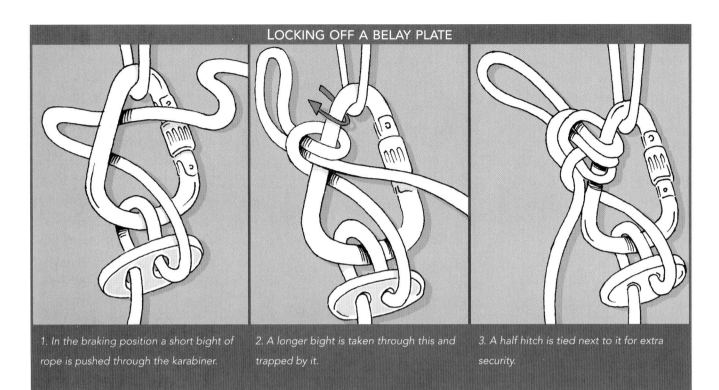

1. In the braking position a short bight of rope is pushed through the karabiner.

2. A longer bight is taken through this and trapped by it.

3. A half hitch is tied next to it for extra security.

A figure eight descender can also be locked off by bringing the dead rope over and jamming it under the live rope. This can be tricky, since you would need to bring the rope past the running position, making it hard to hold the load. It is also difficult to release. It should be backed up with at least one solid hitch around your locking karabiner

SELF-LOCKING BELAY DEVICES

There are a number of self-locking belay devices on the market, all with different degrees of effectiveness and working on slightly different principles. However, they all lock under load. It is advisable to back up this lock-off by tying some hitches around your locking karabiner if you want to release your hands.

FRICTION HITCH

To lock off with a friction hitch is very similar to a belay plate, except here the hitches are made around the live rope rather than the karabiner.

LOCKING OFF WITH A FIGURE EIGHT DESCENDER

Cross the braking rope behind the load rope. This requires further securing since it can slip.

LOCKING OFF WITH A FRICTION HITCH

A further half hitch should be tied to ensure that it cannot come out accidentally.

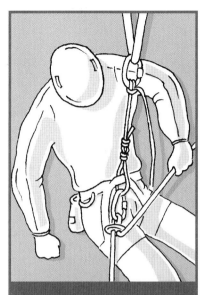

Leader locks off the rope through belay device

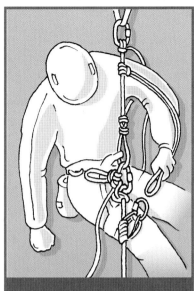

After locking off belay with lock-off knot, the leader connects prusik loop from the anchor to the live rope holding the fallen climber.

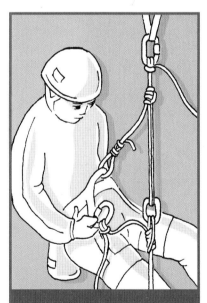

After untying the lock-off, the leader releases the tension on the belay and is now free to untie himself from the system.

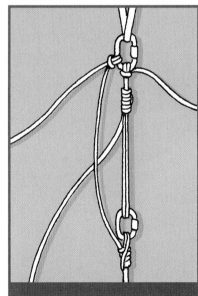

The live rope is connected directly to the anchor before the leader goes for help.

Escaping the system

Escaping from the system entails removing yourself from the belay system and rope while it is under tension. This will be necessary if you need to assist an injured partner hanging from the rope, or if you need to fetch assistance.

Every belay stance and anchor system will demand slightly different ways of going about escaping the system, but once you understand the basics, they can be adapted to most situations.

Step 1. Lock off the belay device to free both hands.

Step 2. Attach a prusik loop to the live rope (the one under tension), preferably using a French Prusik (see *p80*), since this is easier to release under tension than the standard prusik.

Step 3. Connect this prusik loop directly to one of the karabiners on the belay anchor. (Remember to keep the forces in a straight line.) If the karabiners are out of reach, then attach another prusik loop to the rope leading to the belay and connect the two prusik loops.

Step 4. Make sure that the prusik loops are taut, then release the lock-off on the belay device and allow the prusiks to take the full weight of the hanging climber. The belayer has now been totally bypassed.

Step 5. Take the main rope and tie it directly into the anchor using a clove hitch or a figure eight. Never leave a climber hanging supported only by a prusik loop.

Step 6. Now it is possible to untie from the system and abseil (rappel) down to your partner or go for help.

Hoisting

There are several types of hoists and some can be fairly complex, but most work on the same principle. Hoisting systems can be divided into two groups: assisted and unassisted.

ASSISTED HOIST

This system can be used if the person being hoisted is able to assist in the operation and is not more than one third of a rope length below the belayer.

Step 1. Lock off the belay device. Put a French prusik on the live rope just below the belay device and clip the other end of the prusik loop into the belay loop of your harness. Make sure that the loop is not long enough for the prusik knot on the rope to go out of arm's reach.

Step 2. Lower a bight of rope down to the stranded climber who must clip the bight through a locking karabiner attached to the belay loop on the harness.

Step 3. Release the lock-off on the belay device and let the prusik loop take the weight of the stranded climber.

Step 4. The belayer starts to hoist on the third rope while the stranded climber pulls down on the middle rope. The French prusik is held open by the plate as the first rope moves through it, but when a rest is required, simply release the rope; the stranded climber is lowered slightly until the first rope is locked by the prusik knot. Resume hoisting again at any time. All runners (points of intermediate protection through which the climbing rope is run) must be unclipped as the climber is hoisted past them.

Right: Assisted hoist with the rope through the belay plate and the French prusik on the rope to the distressed climber. The latter pulls down on the middle rope (which runs down to him) and the belayer pulls up on the third rope.

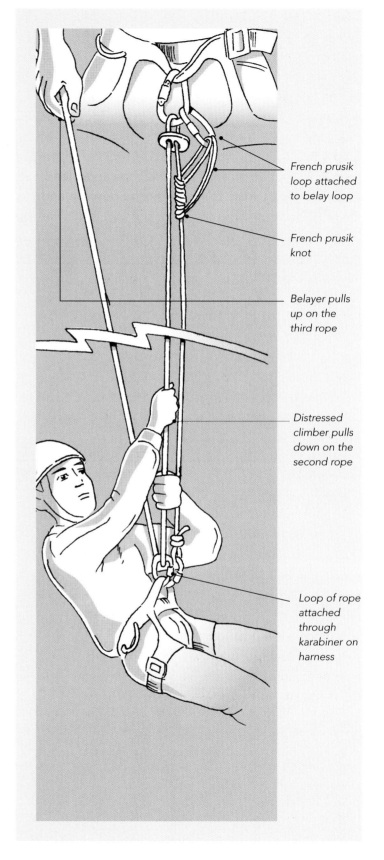

French prusik loop attached to belay loop

French prusik knot

Belayer pulls up on the third rope

Distressed climber pulls down on the second rope

Loop of rope attached through karabiner on harness

UNASSISTED HOIST

There are several types of unassisted hoists that one can put into operation, the most common being the three-in-one hoist, or Z-pulley system. This system should be used if the climber is unable to assist, or when more than one third of a rope-length is below the belayer.

Step 1. Escape from the system (see p179).

Step 2. Attach two prusiks to the the rope under load. One must be as close to the anchor as possible and the other as close to the climber as possible, given the length of the prusik loop and accessibility of the rope itself. The prusik loop used to escape from the system can usually double up for the lower prusik loop on the hoisting rig. The top prusik loop must be attached to the rope with a French prusik, which is then clipped to the anchor.

Step 3. Undo the back-up knot tied when you escaped from the system and let the load rest on the French Prusik. Then thread the rope through the same karabiner to which the French Prusik is attached.

Step 4. Connect a karabiner to the lower prusik loop and clip the rope through that karabiner as well. You are ready to hoist.

Step 5. Now pull up on the rope which runs through the lower karabiner and your load will start to move upwards with a mechanical advantage of 3:1.

As you pull up, the rope runs through the top prusik. When released the prusik locks, preventing the rope from slipping back down. Then the lower prusik is released and pushed back down as far as it can go. This process is repeated until the load is raised.

An important point to remember about all these emergency procedures is that you have to go out there and get some hands-on experience. The more you practise the better and smoother the procedures will become.

Right: Unassisted hoist with a French prusik at the double karabiner pulley at the anchor and a simple prusik knot further down the rope.

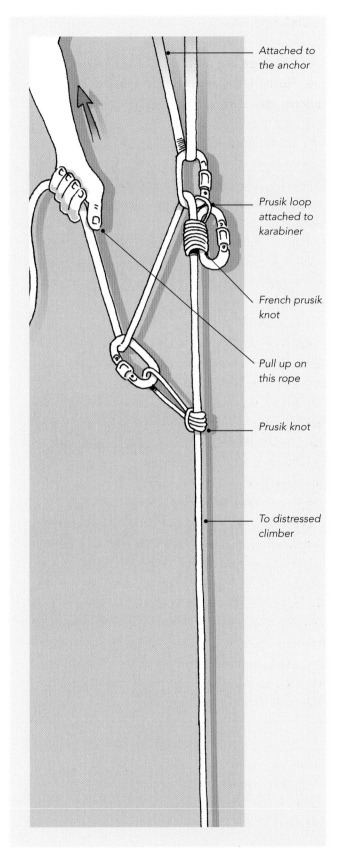

Attached to the anchor

Prusik loop attached to karabiner

French prusik knot

Pull up on this rope

Prusik knot

To distressed climber

Abseil (also rappel): The German word for the technique of descending a rope. Rappel is from the French Both terms are used throughout the world.

Adze Flat scrapping or cutting edge of an ice axe head.

Aid climbing Pitons, bolts and other hardware are used for direct aid when steep and/or blank sections of rock cannot be climbed with conventional free climbing techniques.

Aiders Specially designed stepped slings to stand in while aid climbing.

Anchors The point where a climber attaches themselves to a cliff using natural or artificial anchors.

Arête A narrow, sharp ridge of rock, snow or ice; outward corner.

Arm bar Bracing the arms across an off-width crack as a means of ascending.

Artificial climbing See aid climbing

Ascenders Mechanical clamp-like devices used for ascending a rope.

Back belay A belay arranged for the second to accompany a normal belay from the top, so as to avoid a pendulum.

Bail Retreat, usually off a route.

Balance move A delicate move requiring good balance.

Bandolier A type of sling worn around the neck to rack gear.

Barn-door An uncontrollable outward swing caused by lack of balance, commonly found on laybacks and arêtes.

Base camp The first and largest camp established to climb a mountain expedition style. All activity thereafter stems from this camp.

Bashie Soft aluminium or copper blobs that can be hammered into grooves and scoops for aid climbing.

Bat hook A sharp-tipped hook that can be placed onto tiny edges, or shallow drilled holes in aid climbing.

Belay Procedure of securing a climber by making it possible for the belayer, attached to an anchor, to hold a fall by stopping the rope.

Belay device Device through which the rope is threaded to brake the rope in the event of a fall.

Belay station Stance and anchors used by the belayer while belaying the other climber.

Benighted Caught out in the dark on a mountain.

Bergschrund The gap formed between a receding glacier or ice field and a rock face.

Big wall Any big face higher than 500m (16,000ft), which demands technical free and/or aid climbing, requiring multiday ascents, and huge amounts of gear, food and water to be hauled up the face.

Birdbeak Type of piton with a thin, sharp, hook-like blade used in thin cracks.

Bivouac Overnight camp on a mountain or rock wall during a climb.

Black ice Ice formed directly from freezing ground water, often very hard and glassy.

Blind move A move made where the hold gained cannot be seen at the outset.

Bold A route which has little protection, demanding a brave and confident approach.

Bollard A rounded, protruding piece of rock or ice that can often be used as an anchor. Can be chopped out of a snow slope with an axe.

Bolt A stainless steel expansion bolt or glue-in placed in rock as a permanent anchor point.

Bolt hanger The metal plate fixed to a bolt to allow a karabiner to be clipped to it.

Bombproof Any piece of gear, or anchor system, which is very solid and has no chance of coming out.

Bulge A protruding piece of rock or snow, which is steeper than the surrounding terrain.

Buttress A rock mass that stands proud of the main massif, or mountainside.

Camming device Piece of climbing equipment that jams into cracks. Movable cams are depressed with a trigger mechanism, inserted into a crack, then released, forcing the cam wheels up against the sides.

Campus board A board placed at an overhanging angle against a wall. Hand holds are mounted on the board, which you use to do pull-ups by 'walking' up the rungs.

Chalk Magnesium carbonate, which is used to keep the hands free from sweat, allowing for better grip on small, or sloping holds.

Chimney Fissure in a rock face that is wide enough to allow the whole body.

Chockstone A rock jammed into a horizontal or vertical crack that can be used as an anchor.

Chop Purposefully remove the bolts of a route.

Choss Section of loose or rotten rock.

Clean climbing Climbing a free or aid pitch using hand placed, removable protection that does not damage the rock.

Clean a pitch Removal of gear from a rock pitch.

Clove hitch A knot that is used extensively for securing to anchor points.

Committing A move or pitch that demands a bold approach due to bad or sparse gear.

Contour A line on a map that links all points of equal height.

Copperhead See bashie

Corner A recessed corner, normally with sides near right angles to each other.

Cornice A curved, overhanging ridge of snow formed by the wind.

Couloir French word for gully, which can contain snow, ice or rubble. Prone to avalanches and rock fall.

Cow's tail A length of sling attached to your harness, used for clipping into aid gear.

Crack Any fissure in a rock face.

Crag A small rock wall.

Crank To execute a powerful move by pulling hard on your arms.

Crimpy (of a route) With tiny or thin edges where you can only use the tips of your fingers.

Crux The hardest move or sequence of moves on a pitch.

Deadpoint (in a lunge or dynamic move) The moment of weightlessness at the point where upward movement ceases, but before downward movement starts.

Dead rope Part of the rope that is not under tension, coiled on the ground and not between the belay device and the climber who is climbing.

Delicate Move requiring good balance.

Desperate A very difficult move, or sequence, requiring a reasonably bold approach.

Dihedral See corner.

Direct A route that takes a direct line with little, or no deviation.

Direct aid To use aid while climbing a pitch.

Dome A rounded dome of rock, commonly found in granite rock formations.

Double boot Has a rigid shell and an insulated, removable inner boot.

Double fisherman's knot A knot used for joining two ropes.

Double rope technique A system using double ropes as opposed to a single rope for climbing.

Dyno Dynamic move that requires a lunge to reach the next hold.

Edging To stand on tiny holds or edges while climbing.

Ethics The behaviour of climbers towards rock walls and mountains in general.

Etriers See aiders

Expanding flake A flake that moves or expands when gear is placed behind it.

Exposure Space below the climber (air beneath your feet), a combination of height above the ground and steepness of the rock. Also another name for hypothermia.

Face Crackless, relatively featureless expanse of rock.

Face climbing Free climbing on crackless walls, using edges and various face climbing techniques to maintain balance.

Fall factor Number indicating the severity of a fall, obtained by dividing the length of the fall by the length of rope involved.

Fifi hook Hook tied to the top of an aider to hook directly into the eye of a piton.

Figure-eight descender An abseil device shaped like a figure eight. The rope is threaded through and around it to create friction.

Figure of eight knot Used to tie into harnesses and at anchors.

Fingerboard An artificial board with holds of varying sizes, used for training purposes.

Finger lock The technique used to lock your fingers into a crack as a hold.

First ascent The first time a route has ever been climbed. This is normally recorded.

Fist jam Wedging a fist into a crack by clenching the fist and expanding it.

Fixed protection Protection placed that is not removed.

Fixed rope Ropes fixed in position over sections of a climb to facilitate the continuous climbing, or passing over that section. Normally used during an expedition, or siege tactics on a big wall.

Flake A thin, flat section of rock standing away from the main face.

Flared crack A crack, or chimney that is wider on the outside than the inside.

Flash ascent To climb a route on a first attempt.

Foot hold Any hold used to place the feet.

Free abseil An abseil that leaves the climber hanging free from the surrounding rock walls.

Free ascent Involves no aid climbing

Free climbing Using rope and protection gear only to arrest a fall, but not as direct aid in making height.

French technique Climbing ice and snow by flat-footing with the crampons facing downwards for better grip. The ice axe acts as the third contact point.

Friction climbing Climbing on slabs where no footholds are evident, relying on the friction between the sticky rubber soles and the smooth rock.

Friction hitch See Italian hitch

Friends Trade name of the original spring loaded camming devices invented in the late 1970s.

Front pointing Climbing steep ice or snow using the front points of your crampons.

Gendarme A pillar standing proud of the surrounding mountainside.

Girdle traverse Crossing an entire crag, or cliff.

Glaciers Rivers of ice moving downhill, under the influence of gravity.

Glacier travel The art of moving safely across glaciers and among crevasses.

Glissading A controlled slide down hard snow in a standing, or crouched position, using the ice axe as a brake.

Gore-Tex Trade name for the first breathable waterproof fabric available.

Grades Climbs according to their level of difficulty. Every country and discipline has a separate system.

Grip Any hand or foot hold.

Gripped A state of fear while climbing, mainly due to being run out (see separate entry), or high above the ground.

Groove An open, shallow corner.

Half-rope A rope only suitable for leading when used with another half-rope. (See double rope technique.)

Hand jam Expanding a hand inside a crack, causing it to jam there.

Hanger See bolt hanger

Hanging belay A belay stance without a ledge of any sort to stand on. The belayer simply hangs from the gear placed in the rock.

Heelhook A technique used where the heel is hooked into a hold above the head.

Hexcentric Six-sided nuts that can be cammed or wedged into cracks.

High-altitude climbing Climbing above 7000m (23,000ft).

Hold See grip.

Hooking See skyhook

Ice fall Steep, dangerous area of a glacier, where rapid movement, due to steepness, has caused a chaotic mixture of crevasses and seracs that can collapse at any time.

Incut A positive, sharp-edged hold behind which you can get your fingers.

Italian hitch (also friction hitch) A hitch that can be used in place of a belay or abseil device (see separate entry).

Jamming Wedging hands, feet, arms, knees or legs into a crack as a hold.

Jug Big, positive hold that can be gripped with security. Derived from jug handle.

Jumars See ascenders.

Karabiner, clipgate, snapgate Light-weight aluminium alloy snaplink with a springloaded gate used to connect the rope and slings to the protection gear and anchors.

Karabiner, locking gate As above, but with a gate that locks, to prevent accidental opening.

Kernmantle Standard climbing rope, consisting of a number of braided strands which make up the core (kern), surrounded by a tightly woven sheath (mantle).

Knife edge A sharp horizontal ridge of rock or snow.

Layaway One move of layback technique.

Layback Climbing a crack by gripping an edge with the hands, pulling in one direction, while the feet press against the wall, exerting a force in the opposite direction.

Leader The person who climbs first on a rock climb, or the person who takes the lead role on an expedition or climbing trip.

Leading through When the second finishes a pitch and immediately leads the following pitch.

Line The route up a face or mountain where the climb goes, or where a future climb could go.

Live rope That part of the rope between the belay device and the climber.

Lock off To hold most of your weight on one bent arm while reaching up with the other. Or, to tie off the rope on the belay device, in order to free both hands.

Magnetic variation The difference between true north and magnetic north.

Manky See marginal.

Mantel or mantel shelf Gaining a narrow rock shelf by first pulling up on it until you can push down to waist level, swing one foot onto the shelf and finally stand up.

Marginal A piece of gear that is highly suspect, or an aid placement that will take no more than body weight.

Massif An entire mountain mass.

Micronut Tiny wire nuts used in small cracks.

Mixed climbing Involves snow and rock.

Moraine Boulders and old ice deposited at the snout of a glacier.

Move When a climber moves from one set of holds to another.

Munter hitch See Italian hitch.

Nailing The process of aid climbing a crack or seam with pitons.

Natural line A fault, crack system, or natural weakness on a cliff or peak.

Natural protection Protection that can be placed and removed, leaving the rock face 'clean'.

Neve Snow surfaces that have been hardened due to thawing and freezing.

Nose A protrusion of rock.

Nuts A collective term for all kinds of metal wedges.

Nut tool Used to loosen nuts that are stuck.

Off hand A crack too wide for finger locks, but too narrow for hand jams.

Off width A crack too wide for hand jams, but too narrow for conventional chimney techniques.

On-sight ascent To climb a route without prior knowledge, or ever having seen anyone climbing the route.

Open book See corner.

Overhang A protrusion of rock pushing beyond the vertical, normally in the form of a roof.

Overlap A small overhang or protrusion not necessarily beyond the vertical.

Palming Pushing the hands against holdless rock, to achieve grip through friction.

Peg A metal spike with an eye on one end that is hammered into a crack for protection or used for aid climbing. They come in a variety of sizes and shapes to accommodate different sized cracks.

Pendulum To purposefully swing across a cliff to gain a separate line. Also falling off and swinging across a face.

Pillar A slender column of rock standing proud of a rock face, but not necessarily free standing.

Pinch grip A kind of hold that requires to be pinched between fingers and thumb.

Pinnacle Similar to a pillar, but free standing with a definite summit.

Piolet A standard alpine ice axe.

Pitch The length climbed between two stances or belays.

Piton See peg.

Placement Piece of gear placed as protection or as part of an anchor.

Plastic In ice climbing refers to perfect condition of the ice when near melting point.

Pocket A little hollow in the rock which can be used as a finger hold.

Portaledge Portable ledge with attached tent, that can be anchored to steep cliffs for sleeping on.

Pre-placed Gear placed as protection prior to leading a route.

Protection Gear used to arrest a fall.

Prusik Ascending a rope using prusik loops attached to the rope with a prusik knot.

Prusik knot Friction knot invented by Austrian Dr Karl Prusik that can be moved up, but is locked by a downward force.

Psych out Lose mind control on a route.

Psych up Mentally prepare for a route by positive thinking.

Pumped A term used to describe loss of strength in the arms due to steep, strenuous climbing.

Quickdraw A short, sewn sling with a karabiner at each end used for clipping gear and bolts. Originally a trade name for a type of short sling.

Rack A selection of gear to be used on a climb.

Rail (Break) Horizontal crack that can be used by the hands.

Ramp A low-angle slab usually running through steeper rock, affording a passage.

Rappel See abseil.

Rating systems See grades.

Red point ascent Lead a route cleanly after rehearsing the moves.

Recess Any depression in a cliff. Also see corner.

Rib A thin protuberance on a cliff or mountain face.

Ridge The crest of a mountain, or where two mountain faces meet.

Rock over A high step, where the body weight has to be shifted over the foot to be able to balance up.

Rope drag The friction caused by the rope running against rock and/or at opposing angles.

Rope length The length of a standard climbing rope. Usually 50–60m (150–200ft).

RP The original brass wired nut.

Running belay Another name for any protection placed between two belay stances.

Run out A term which implies that a pitch has little protection. Or when a climber is high above the last piece of protection.

RURP Realised Ultimate Reality Piton, the smallest peg, about the size of a postage stamp. Rurps were developed in 1959 on Kat Pinnacle in Yosemite by Yvon Chouinard to handle the climb's crux, a hairline crack.

Saddle A broad neck between two mountain masses.

Sandbag A climb that is harder than it appears. To deceive a climber into trying a route by saying it is easier than it really is.

Safety rope Rope used as a back-up.

Scrambling Simple climbing, normally not necessitating the use of a rope.

Scree Loose boulders and rocks lying on a slope beneath a cliff.

Sea stack A pillar of rock protruding from the sea. A famous example is the Old Man of Hoy in Scotland.

Second The climber who follows the leader on a pitch.

Self-arrest To stop yourself while falling down a snow slope.

Serac Ice tower which could collapse suddenly.

Shake out Relieving stress on the arms and regaining strength by shaking the arms out while resting.

Side pull A vertical hold on which to pull sideways.

Siege To climb a route using fixed ropes, over a period of time.

Skyhook A metal hook which is placed behind flakes and on tiny edges to hold body weight.

Slab A low angled face.

Sling A sewn loop of webbing used to extend anchor points, or runners

Smearing Stand or make progress on smooth rock, relying on friction alone.

Snow stake An aluminium stake hammered into the snow as an anchor.

Spectra (Dyneema) Trade name for very strong cord or tape.

Speed climbing Climbers trying to climb routes as fast as possible. Also done in competitions.

Sport climbing Climbing fully bolt-protected climbs.

Spot To 'watch' a boulderer while trying a problem. To prevent a bad landing while bouldering.

Stack To press or wedge two or more things together to form a wider and stronger fit in a crack. Fingers, hands, feet, pegs and nuts can be stacked.

Stance A ledge or place where the leader will stop to place an anchor to bring up the second.

Static move A controlled move requiring strength.

Static rope A rope with low stretching properties. Not suitable for leading.

Stemming To exert force with the hands and feet in opposite directions. Typically used when climbing corners (open book).

Stopper move A single very hard move on a pitch of otherwise easier moves.

Sustained Pitch with moves all of a similar grade.

Swing leads See alternate leads.

Talus Another name for scree

Tape The webbing used for slings.

Taping up To tape the fingers to reinforce the tendon pulleys.

Technical Climbing moves at a difficult level.

Tension traverse A climbing traverse using tension from the rope for aid.

Thin Difficult climbing on small holds.

Thread A gap in the rock through which a sling can be threaded.

Three-point contact The principle that states a climber should have three points of contact with the rock while moving a fourth to a new hold.

Tie off Reducing the leverage on pitons that have not been sunk to the hilt in a crack by moving the force closer to the rock.

Tight rope Give assistance to the second by pulling up hard on the rope.

Topo A diagram of a crag or climb showing the route/s with illustrations and symbols rather than in writing.

Top-roping Where a climber climbs a pitch while being belayed with the rope from above.

Traverse Climb sideways.

Tri-cam Passive camming unit used in pockets and rails

UIAA Union Internationale des Associations d'Alpinisme. The European body that determines specifications for climbing equipment and makes policy on matters pertaining to mountaineering.

Undercling Move where the climber grabs the underside of a flake or overhang and uses it to lean out on.

Undercut Where a rock face doesn't go all the way to the ground, leaving a gap between the ground and the start of the cliff.

Verglas A thin, hard layer of ice which forms over rocks when moist air freezes suddenly as it hits frozen rock.

Via ferrata Mountain routes that use chains, cables and ladders to enable hikers and scramblers to access spectacular parts of the mountain.

Wall A big expanse of rock or mixed mountain face.

Waterfall climbing Climbing on frozen waterfalls and large seeps.

Webbing See tape.

Wire A nut or wedge on a wire cable.

Wired When you have all the moves of a route memorized and can climb it with little effort.

Yosemite Valley One of the world's premier rock climbing areas since the 1950s. Situated in California, USA.

Yo-yo A tactic used in climbing where a leader lowers off the highest piece of gear after a fall, then top-ropes back to that point and leading on until eventually succeeding.

Zawn A rocky inlet or amphitheatre set into sea cliffs.

Z-Pulley A type of hoisting system which creates a 3:1 mechanical advantage.

FURTHER READING

Eating for Sport – A Practical Guide to Sports Nutrition by Shelley Meltzer and Cecily Fuller. New Holland, London 2005
Knots – A Complete Guide by Lindsey Philpott. New Holland, London 2004
Top Climbs of the World by Garth Hattingh. New Holland, London 1999
The Games Climbers Play by Ken Wilson. Menasha Ridge Press, Birmingham AL 1978
Ice: Tools and Techniques by Duane Raleigh. Elk Mountain Press, Carbondale CO 1995
The Handbook of Climbing by Allen Fyffe and Iain Peter. Pelham Books, London 1995
How to Rock Climb! by John Long. Falcon Press, Helena Montana 1998

PHOTOGRAPHIC AND ILLUSTRATION CREDITS

All photography by IOL/Mark Johnston, with the exception of the photographs listed below. (Copyright rests with the photographers and/or their agents.) All illustrations by Richard Smith, with the exception of those listed below. (Copyright rests with Images of Africa (www.imagesofafrica.co.za).

Key to Locations: t = top; b = bottom; l = left; r = right; c = centre. (No abbreviation is given for pages with a single image, or pages on which all photographs are by the same photographer.)

ACPL = Alpine Club Photo Library, AH = Andrew Haliburton, AI/GT = Auscape International/Glenn Tempest, BD = Black Diamond, BH = Bill Hatcher, CW = Clinton Whaits, DB = Dermot Brogen, DMM = DMM, GB = Grant Buckley, GE = Greg Epperson, GH = Garth Hattingh, IOA = Images of Africa (www.imagesofafrica.co.za), JC = John Cleare, MT = Maarten Turkstra, DJV = Danie Jansen van Vuuren, DN = Danie Nel, NA = Nicholas Aldridge, NC = Neil Corder, SF = Steven Felmore, P = Petzl, PA = Photo Access, PJ = Peter Janschek, RW = Ray Wood/SC = Simon Carter, CW = Clinton Whaits, JE = Juan Espi, SkC = Ska Cilliers, TL = Tony Lourens

Front cover main ....SC	17 t ....BH	47 cb ....DMM	126 ....DB	156 l & r ....BD
Front cover right (from top) ......AH, AI/GT, AH	17 b ....SkC	48 b.......................BD	127 ....GE	156 c ....GE
	18.............................JC	49 t ....JC	129 ....TL	157 ....GE
Spine ....AI/GT	19 ....ACPL	49 b.......................BD	130.................IOA/CW	158 ....BD
Back cover t........ACPL	20 c ....IOA/JE	55 ....DB	131 b........................BD	159 l ....PJ
Back cover c ....JC	21 ....TL	61 b ....IOA/CW	132 tl ....IOA/CW	159 r ....BD
1 ....DB	24.............................JC	75 ....CW	133 ....MJ	162 c ....JC
3............................JC	28.................IOA/JE	76–78 ....IOA/NC	136 l & r..................JC	165 t ....NA
4 ....SC	30.............................JC	79 r ....IOA/NC	136 c ....CW	165 c & b ....IOA/DN
6 l & r.....................JC	31 ....TL	80–81 l ....IOA/NC	137 ....BH	167–168....................JC
6 c ....DB	32.............................JC	82 ....IOA/JE	138 ....JC	169 ....IOA/CW
7 ....JC	36 c ....BD	84 bl & br ....P	139 ....CW	176 l & r ....IOA/NC
8 l & r ....BH	39 ....BD	85 ....DB	140 l.........................JC	176 c ....BD
8 c.......................ACPL	40 ....GE	92 ....DB	140 r.........................TL	
9............................JC	41 t ....BD	95.................IOA/CW	141.............................JC	
10 ....ACPL	41 c ....IOA/JE	102 t ....JC	142 l & r.................CW	
11 ....SC	41 b ....SC	102 b ....IOA/JE	142 c ....IOA/CW	
12 ....MT	43 t ....DB	107–108...............JC	143 ....GH	**ILLUSTRATIONS**
13 ....ACPL	43 c & b ....BD	109 l.........................TL	144–145..........IOA/CW	23......................IOA/SF
14............................JC	44 t & bl ....BD	109 r ....JC	146 ....CW	27 ....GB
15 ....MT	45 t, cr, b ....BD	110 b ....SC	147 ....JC	29......................IOA/SF
16 t.........................RW	46 ....DB	121 ....MT	148–149 ....ACPL	171 ....IOA/DJV
16 b.........................BH	47 ct.......................BD	122–125 ....JC	153–155 ....JC	174 ....IOA/DJV